Little Birds
Europe
Coloring Book

Pietrangelo Michele

Note

Welcome to this coloring book, thanks for this choice,
I introduce myself, my name is **Michele Pietrangelo** i am an artist, i started drawing and coloring with books from an early age and like you I love coloring books, in my life i bought many, but not all of them were beautiful some with flaws and for this reason that i created one as I liked it with my works more professional and fun way.

How the coloring book is composed:

- The coloring drawing boards are single pages, and have no content behind the image,
- The subjects are free from the background,
- You can create the setting of the subject,
- You can cut out the drawing boards and frame them in a picture,
- There is a blank page between the drawing boards so the color will not pass,
- You can also trace the images with carbon paper or make your drawings,
- Age Range 14 - 100

Instruction to coloring

- You decide to color the subjects,
- Easy With the scientific name find them online, You will find where the subjects live and the colors they have,
- Color the subjects and pass over the outlines later,
- Insert a card under the table before you start coloring,
- Cut out the colored drawing boards and hang them in a beautiful frame,
- Finally you can show me your masterpieces on **Instagram** by tagging me with
  @ michele.pietrangelo.ph I will like it.
- If you have any suggestions for improvement, write me please, i wish you are satisfied.

All © right reserved by michelepietrangelo.com
Book desing, illustration, image, any ideas by Michele Pietrangelo
reproduction is prohibited without rights

Author

Michele Pietrangelo Artist and Photographer. Over 20 years in the world of the image. I did the graphic arts school in Bologna, Italy. I started working in 1995 as a FreeLance, with film camera, going digital. I work with photo agencies, my images are published in magazines and websites all over the world. I help people improve their images in post production and excution. I worked as a consultant in the creation of books on Post Production Photo and Photography Technique

- Web: www.michelepietrangelo.com
- Ig: @michele.pietrangelo.ph
- Fb: michele pietrangelo photograpgy

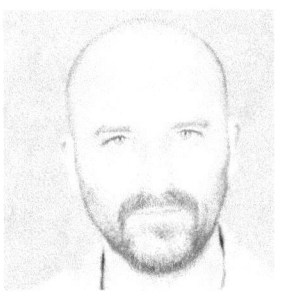

Serinus serinus - Male

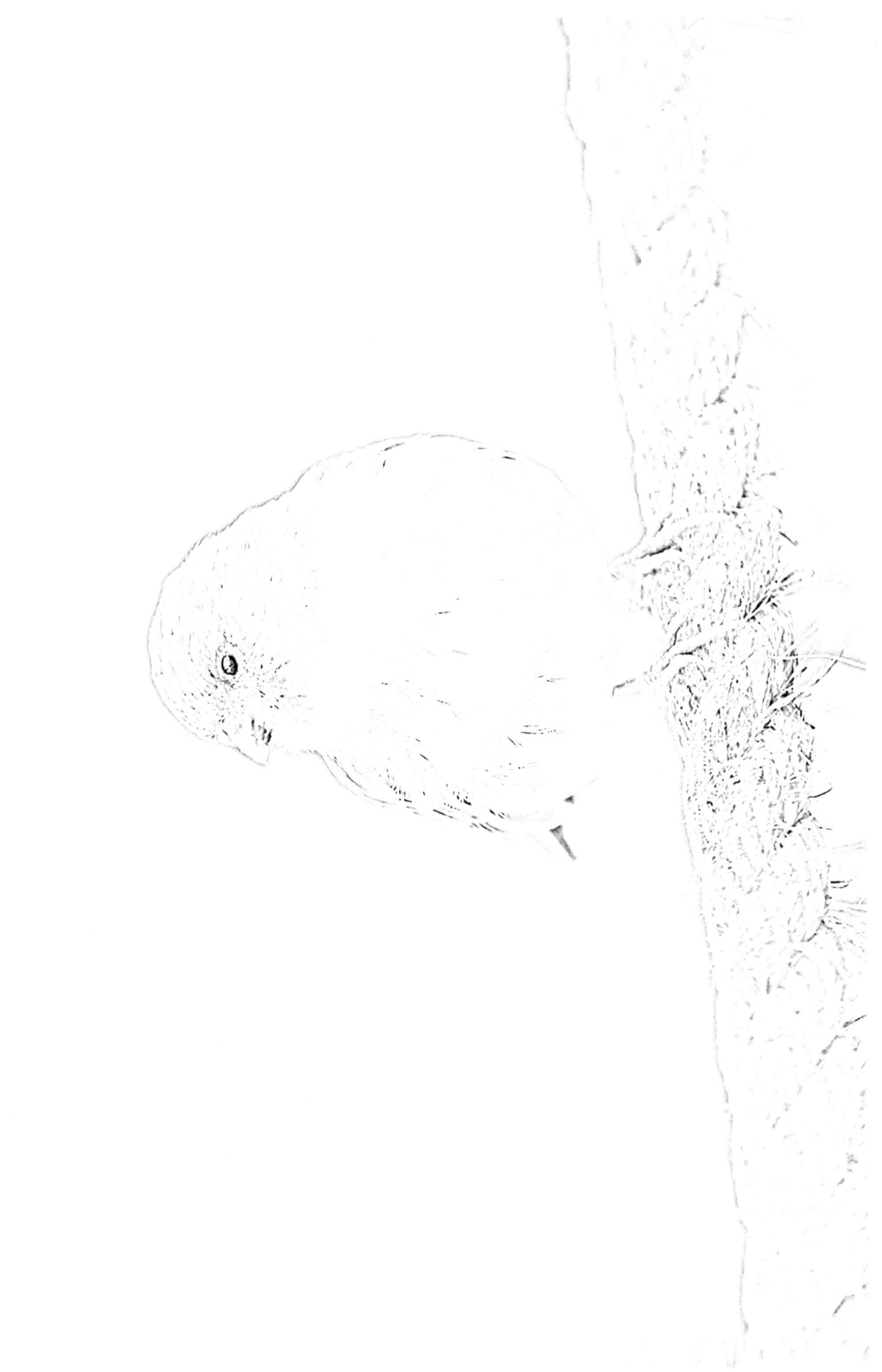

Bombycilla garrulus - Male

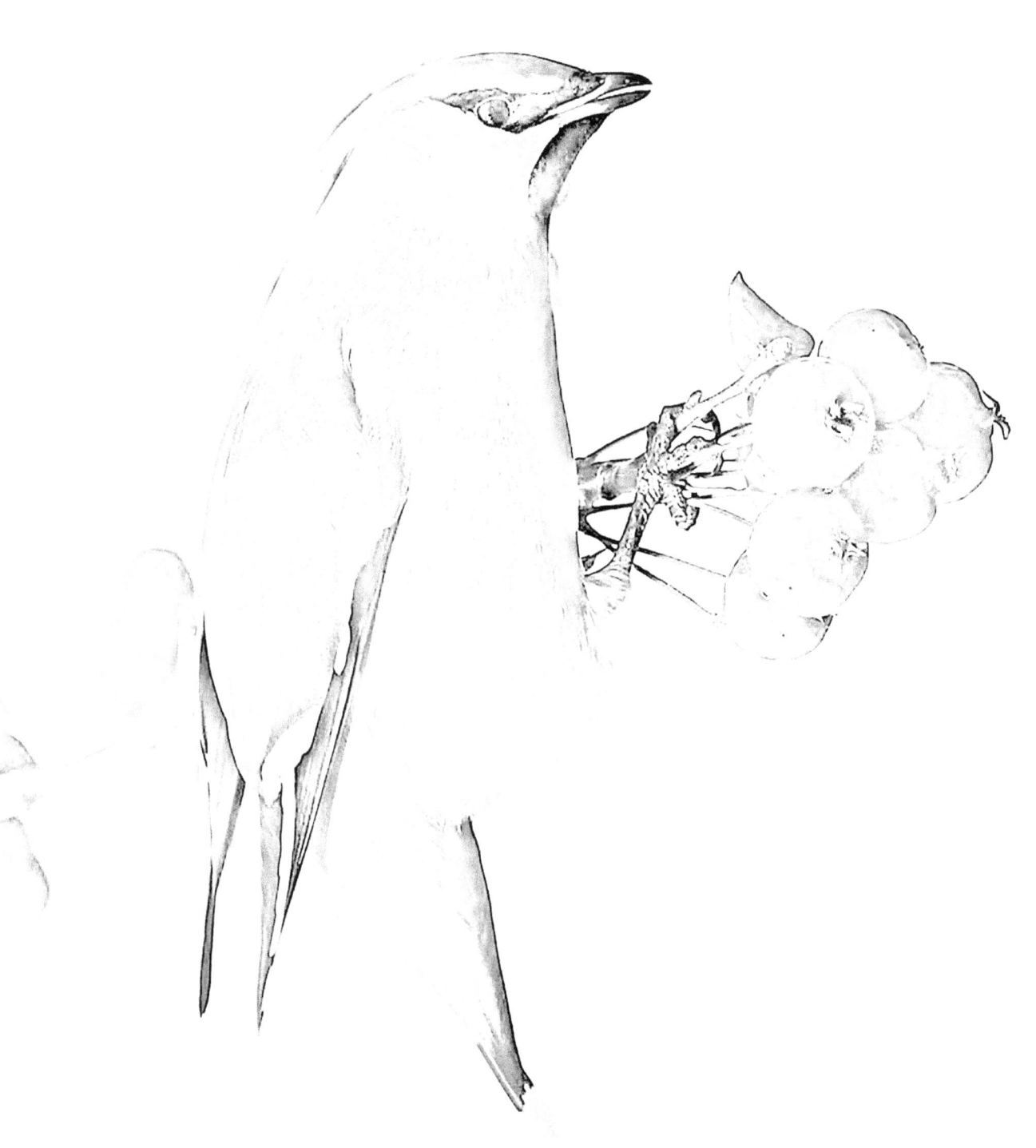

Cinclus cinclus - Male

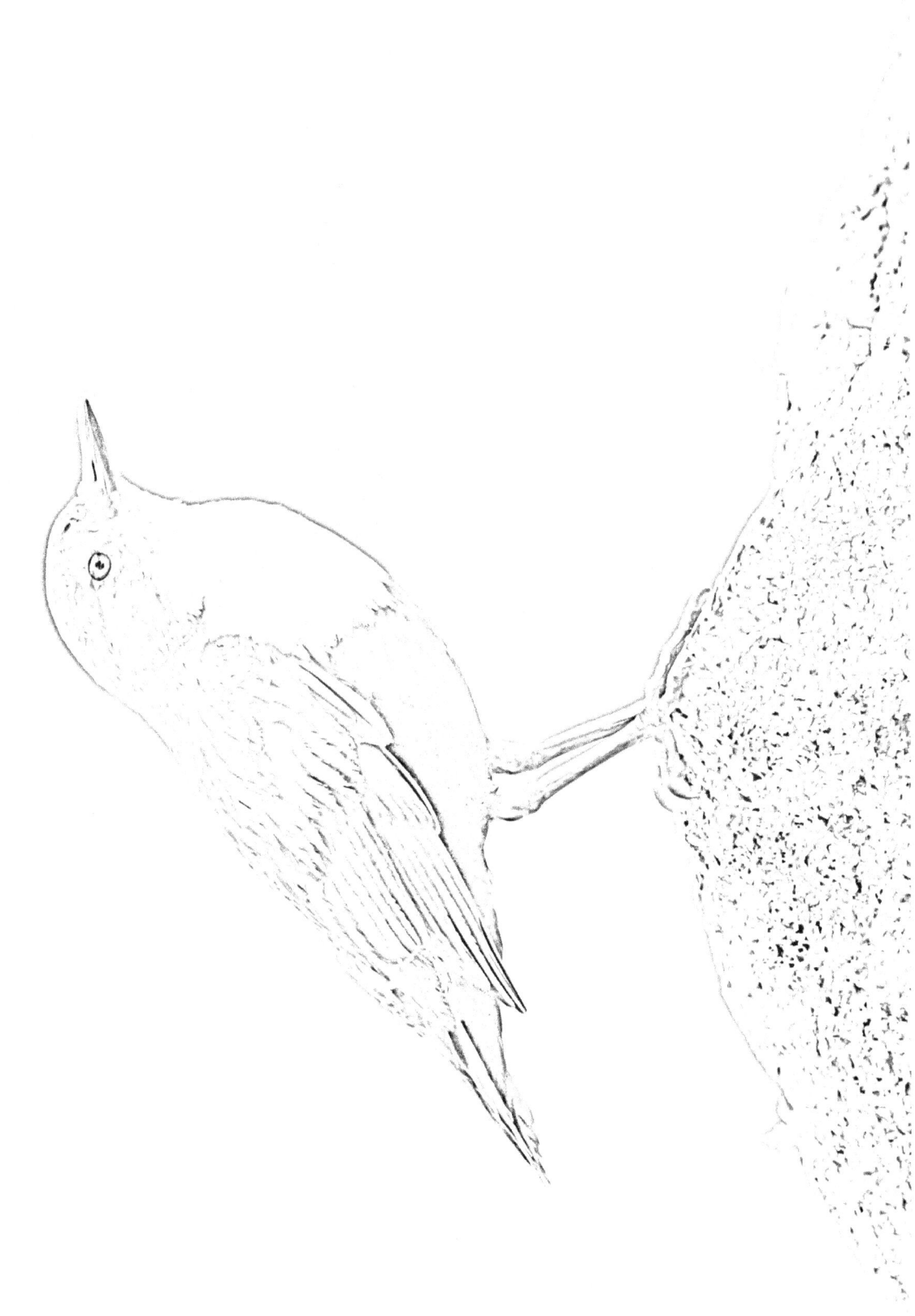

Acrocephalus arundinaceus - Male

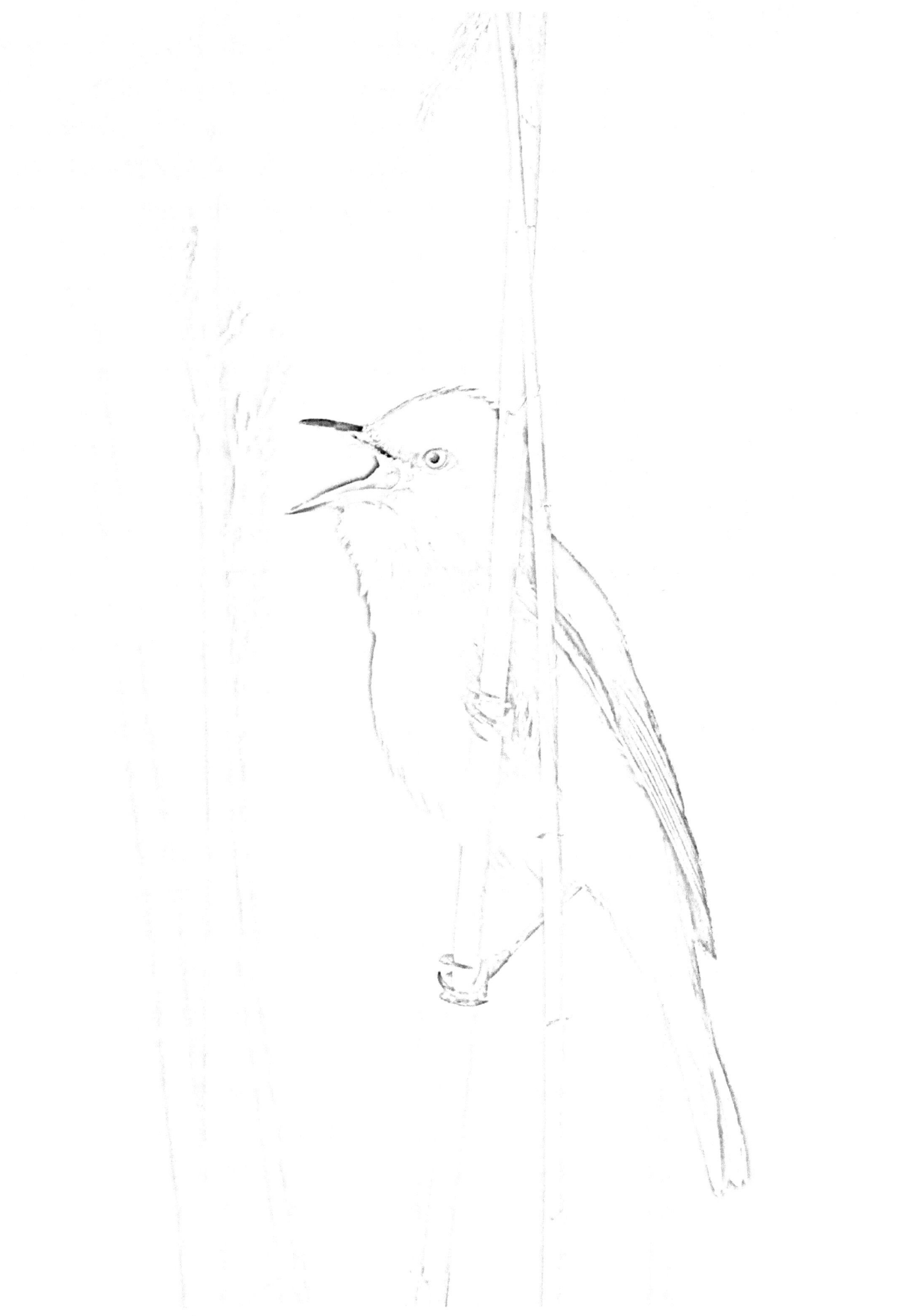

Galerida cristata - Male

Galerida cristata - Male

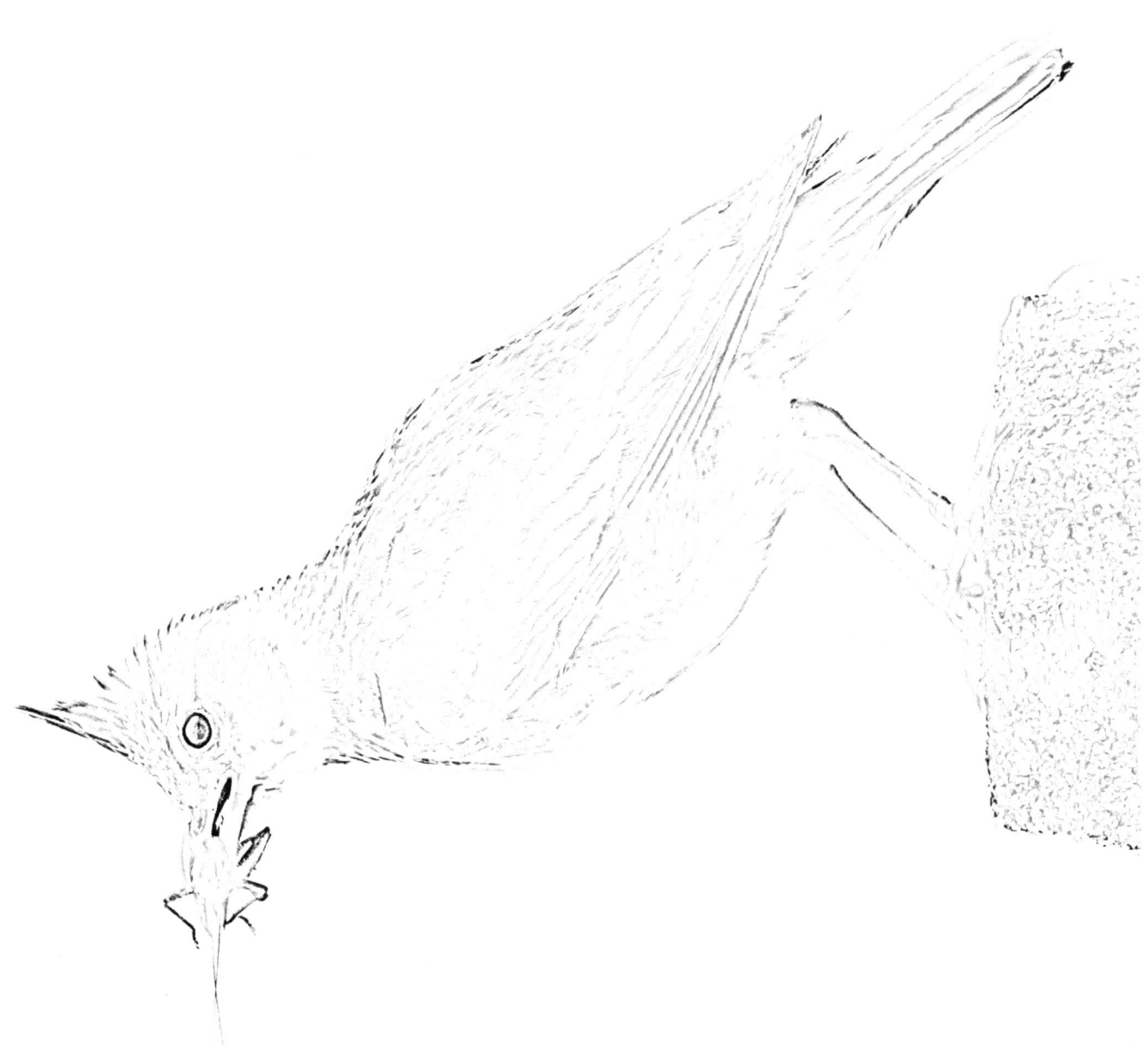

Carduelis carduelis - Male

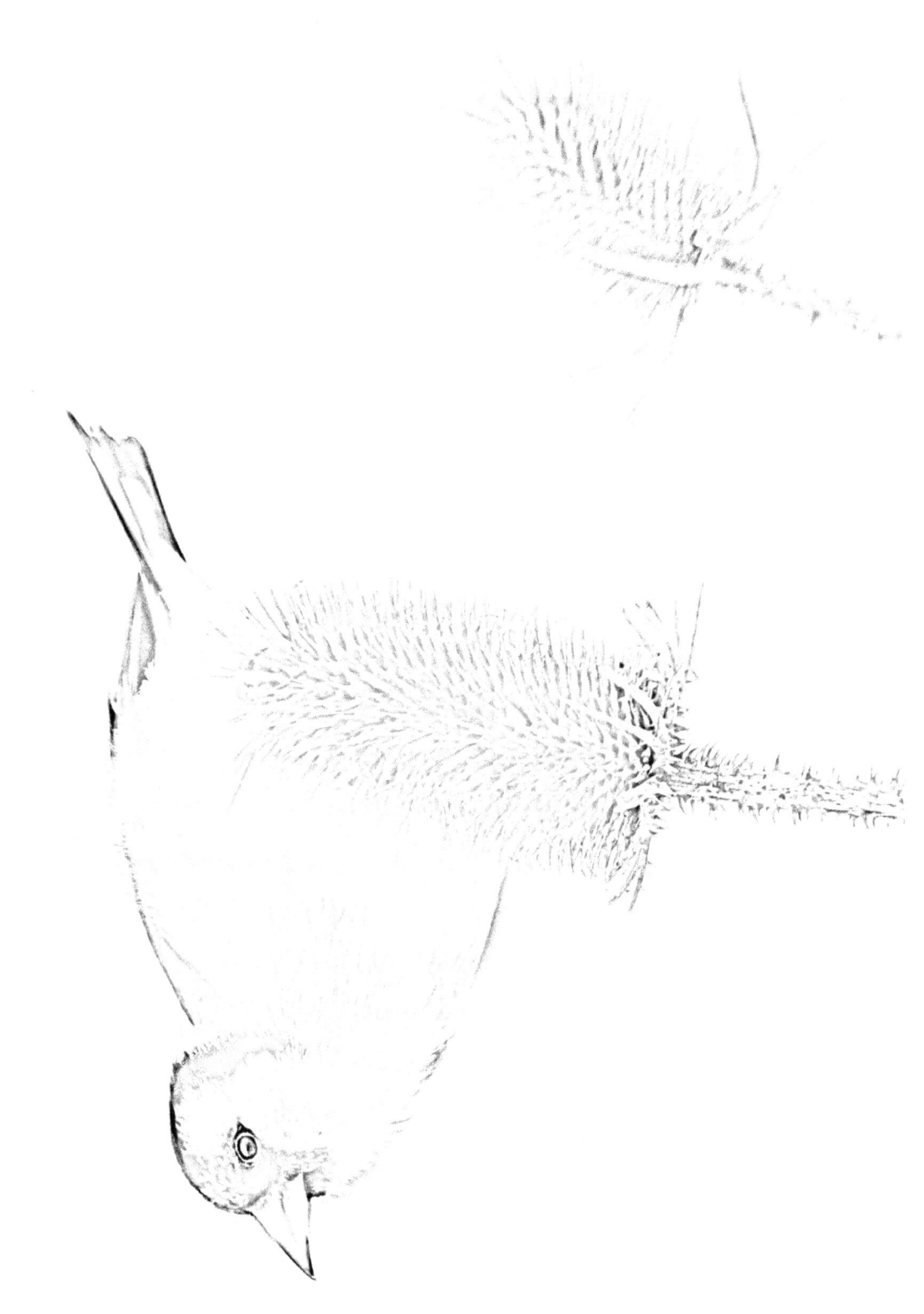

Lophophanes cristatus - Male

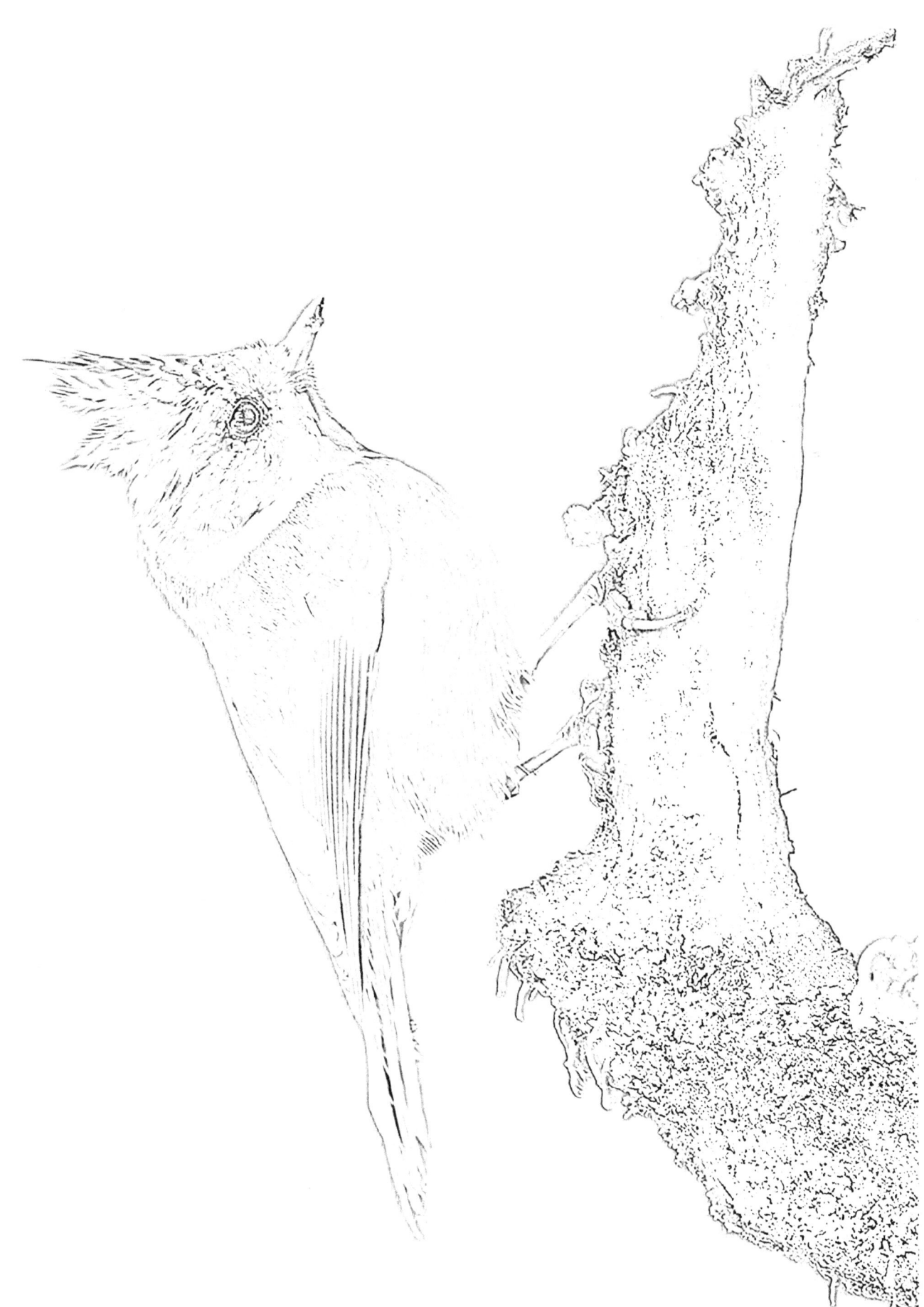

Poecile palustris - Male

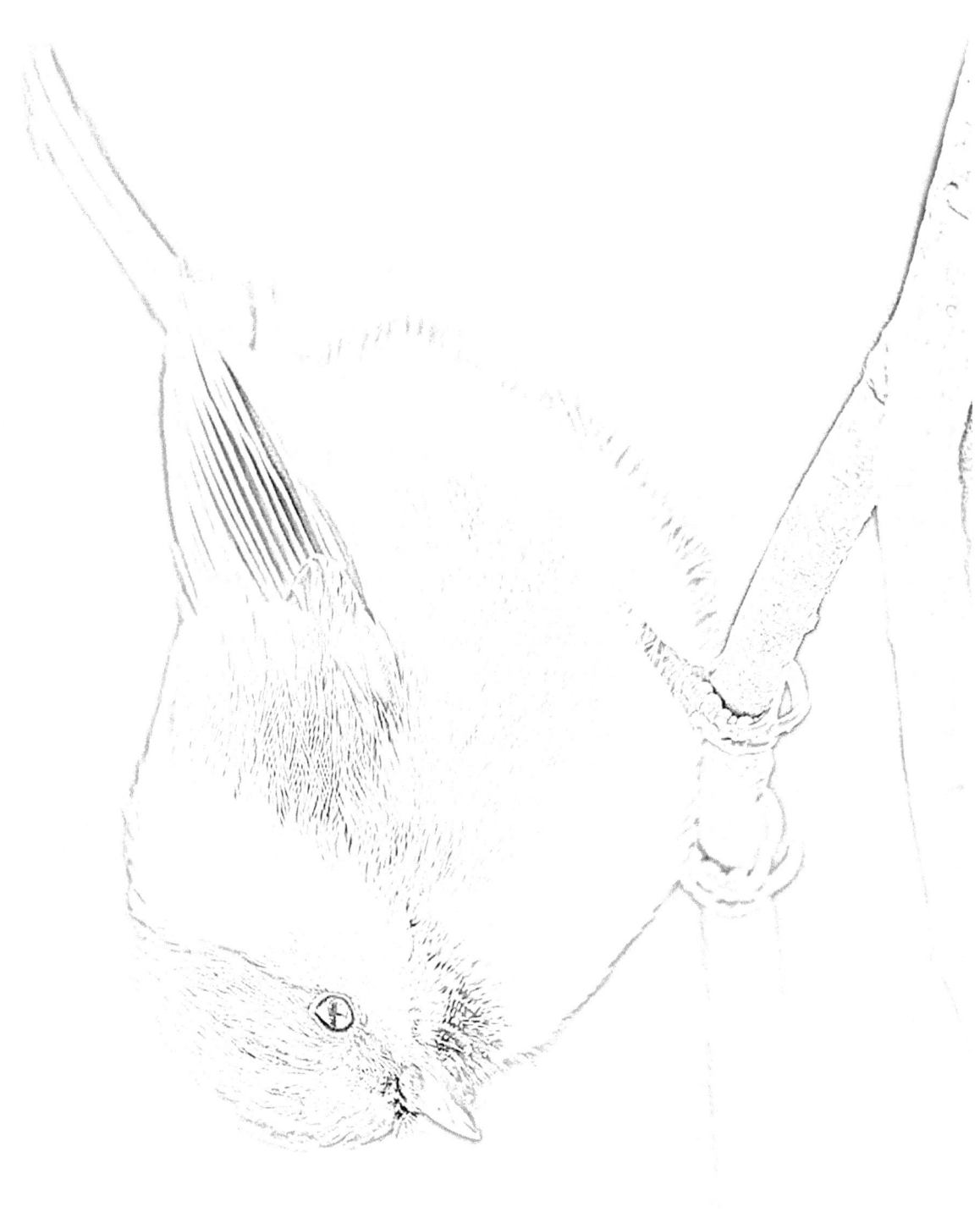

Parus major - Male

Parus major - Male

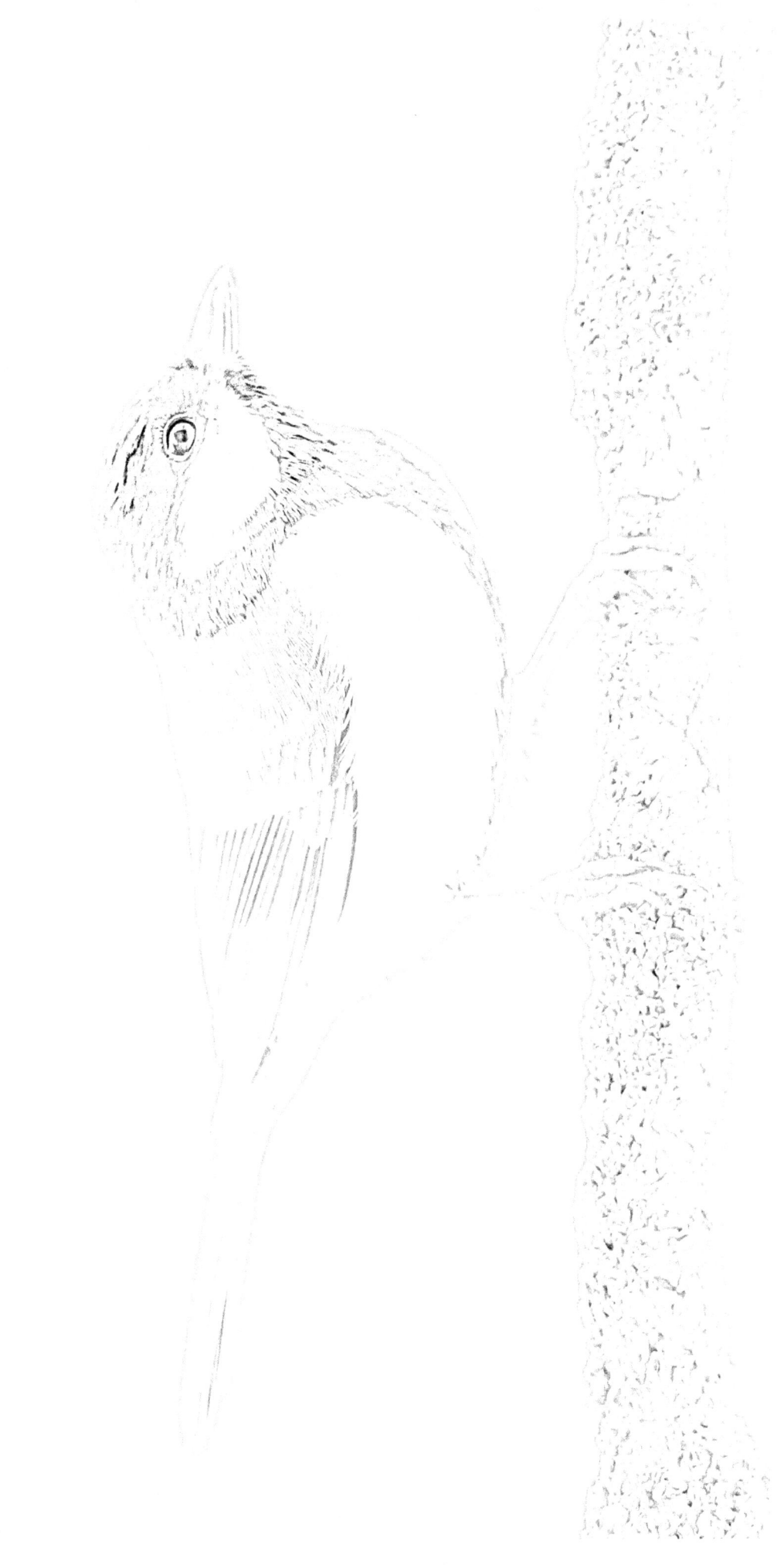

Cyanistes caeruleus - Female

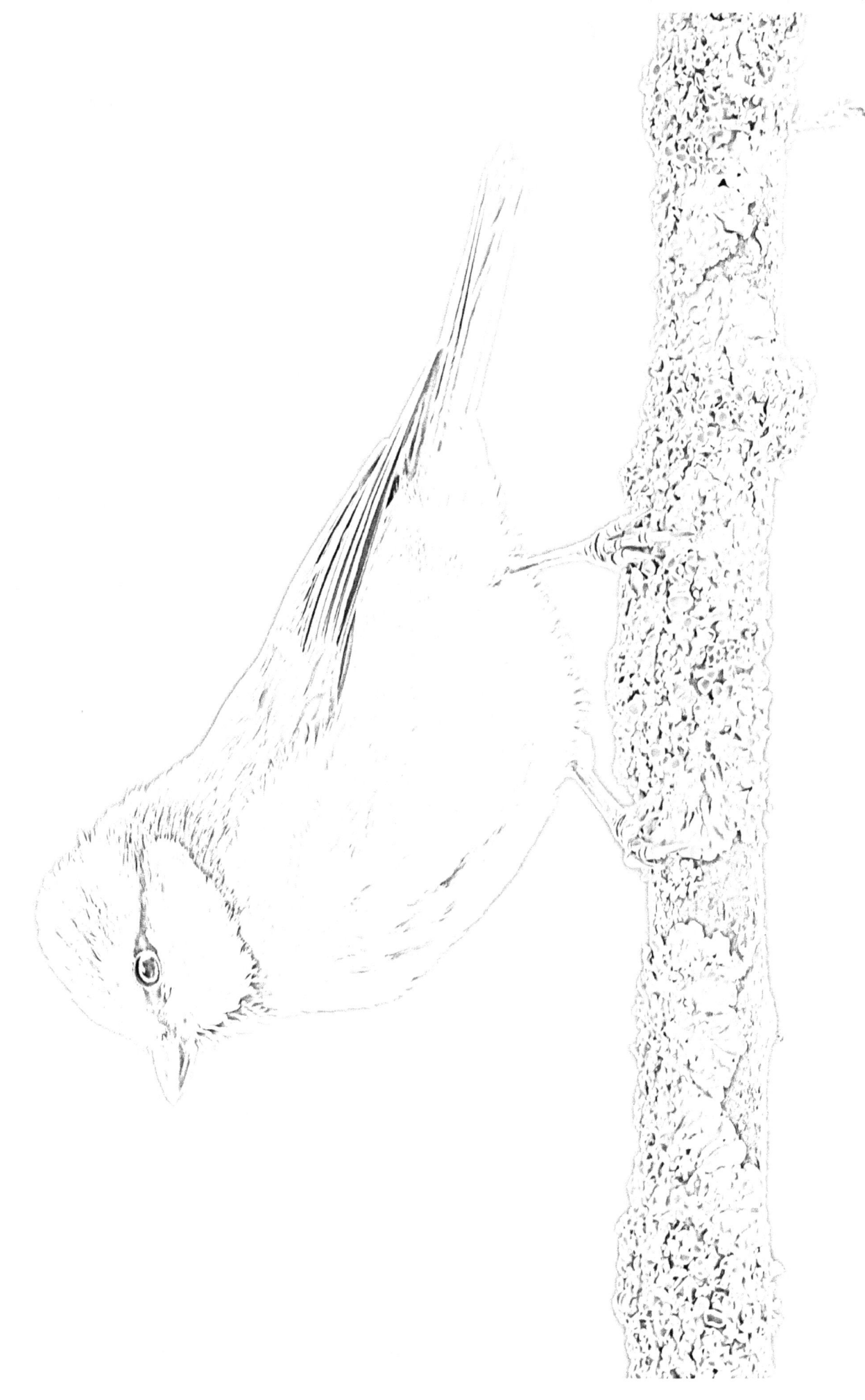

Pyrrhula pyrrhula - Male

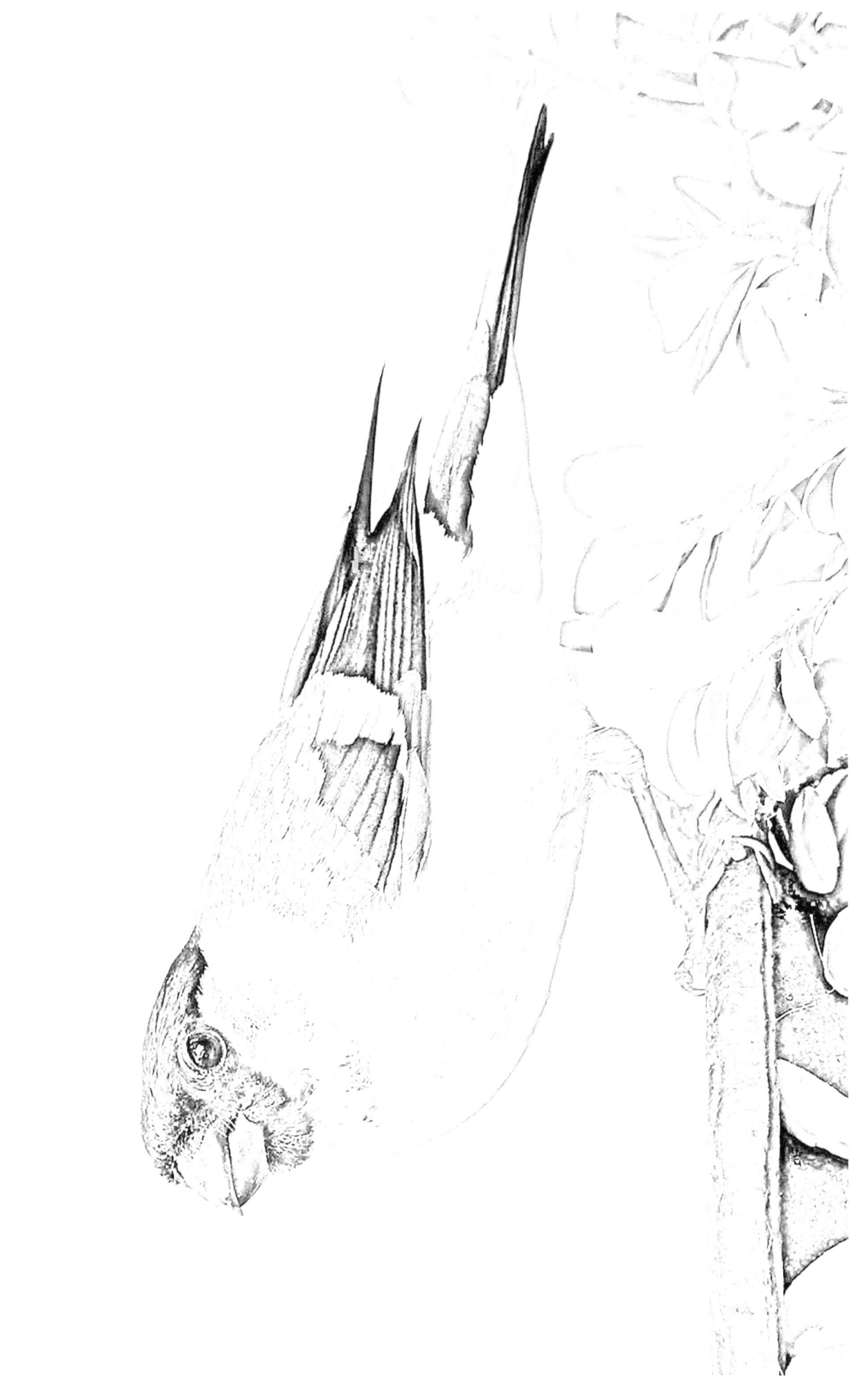

Motacilla flava - Male

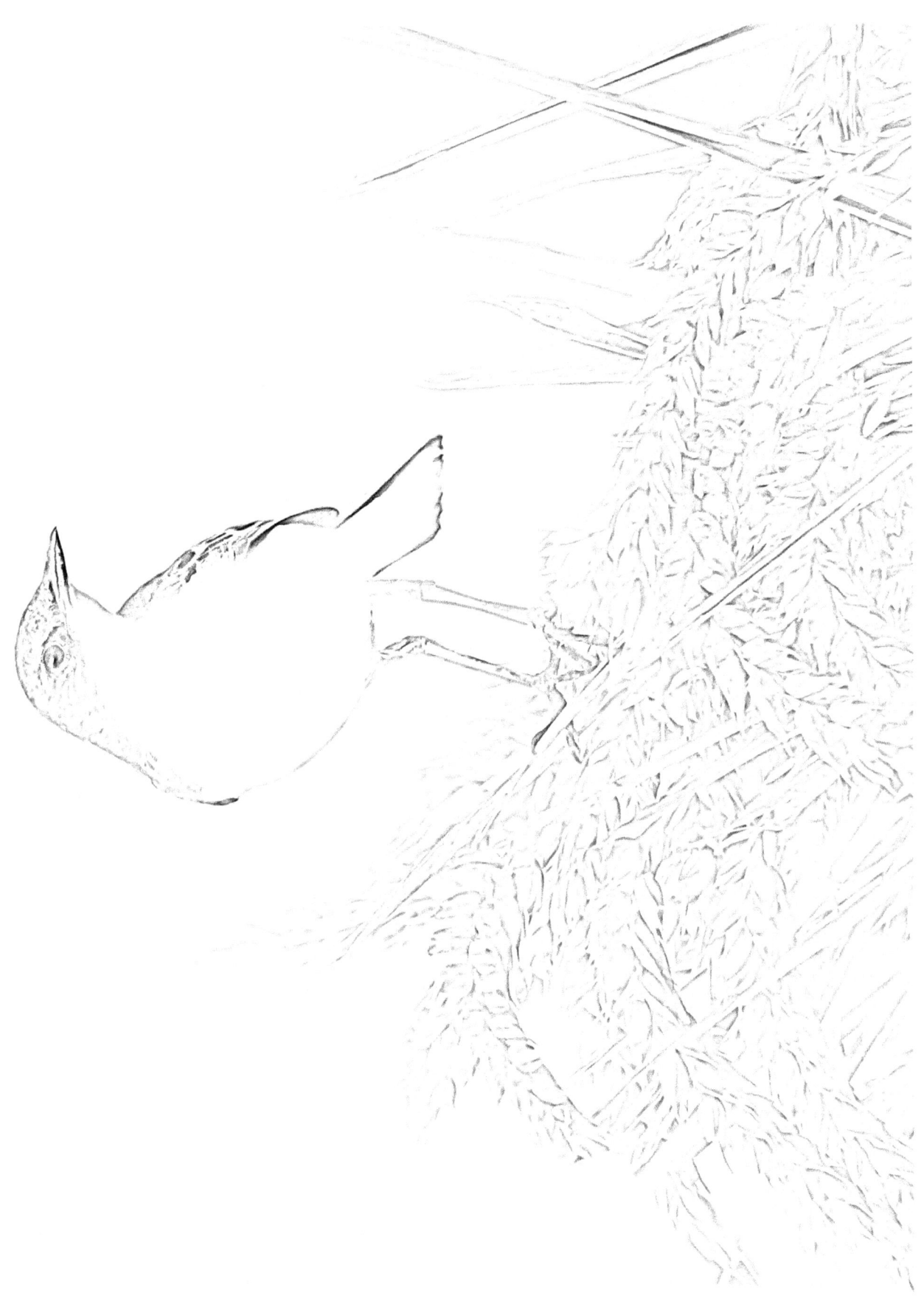

Coracias garrulus - Male

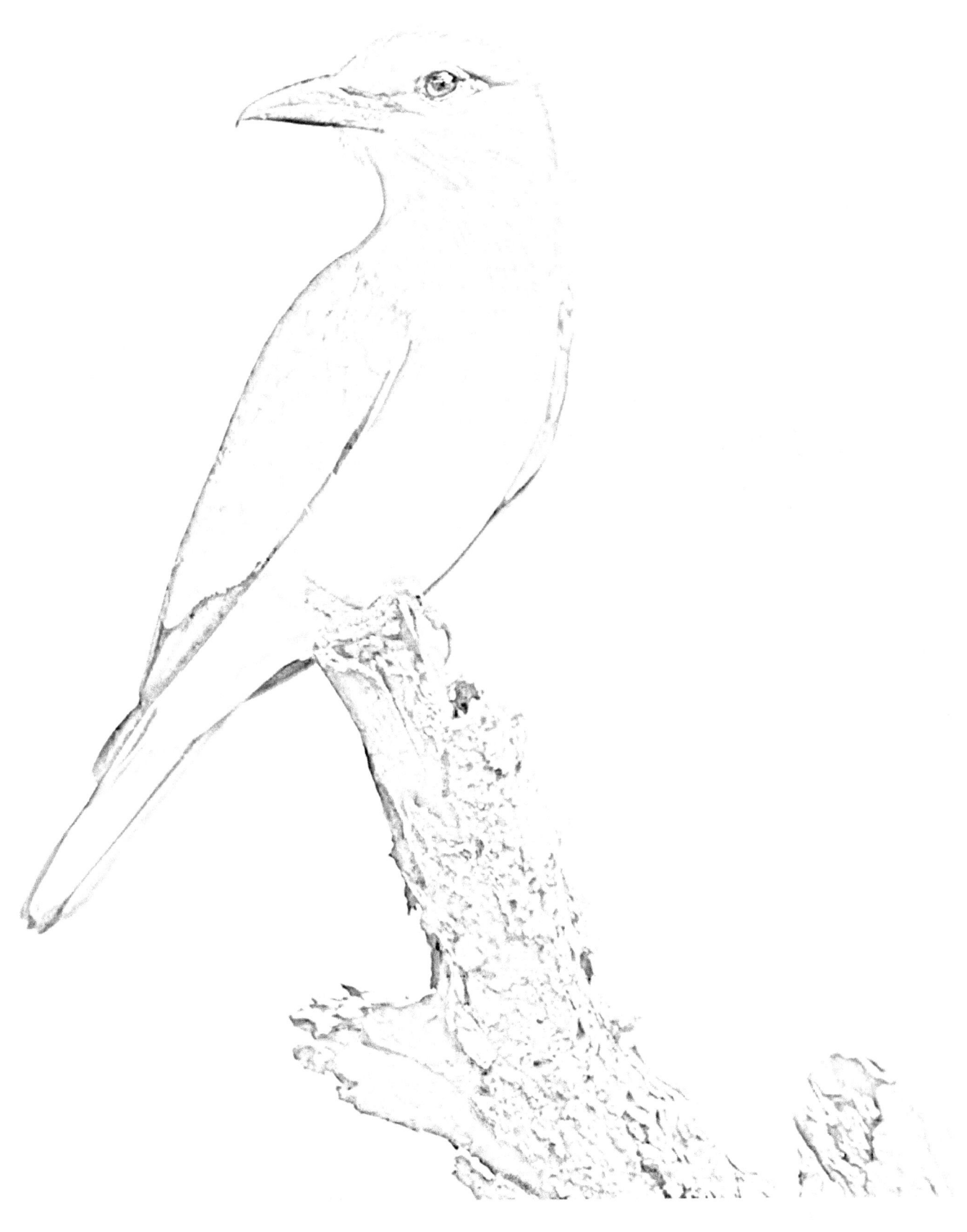

Montifringilla nivalis - Male

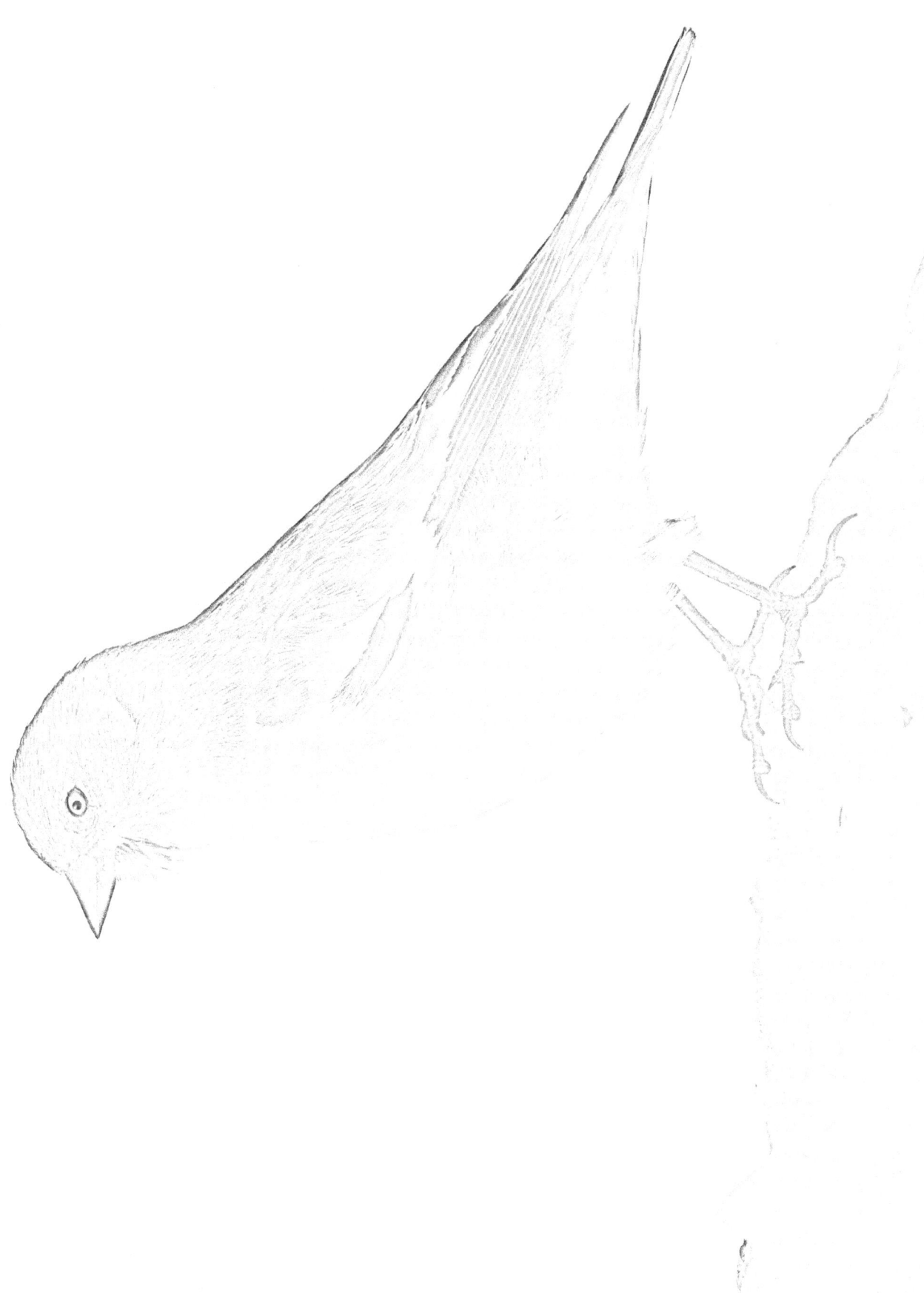

Fringilla coelebs - Male

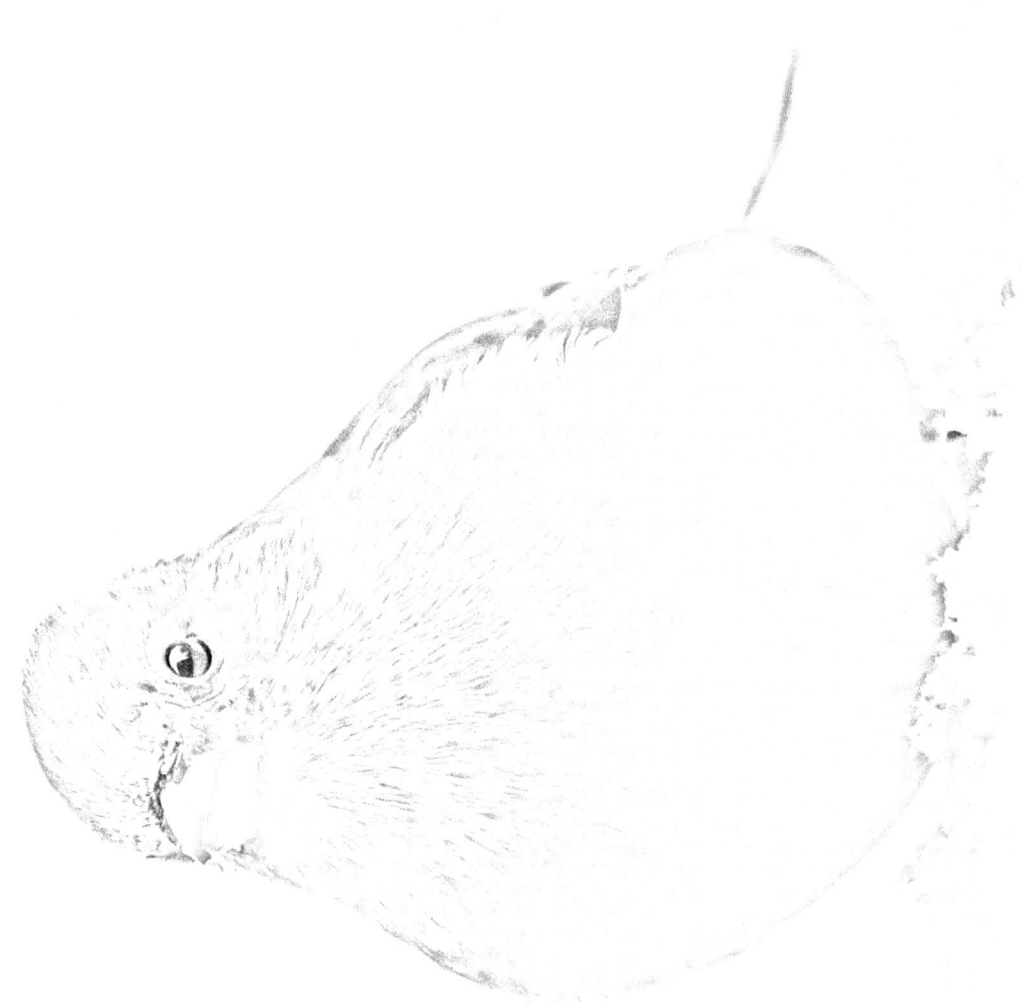

Merops apiaster - Male

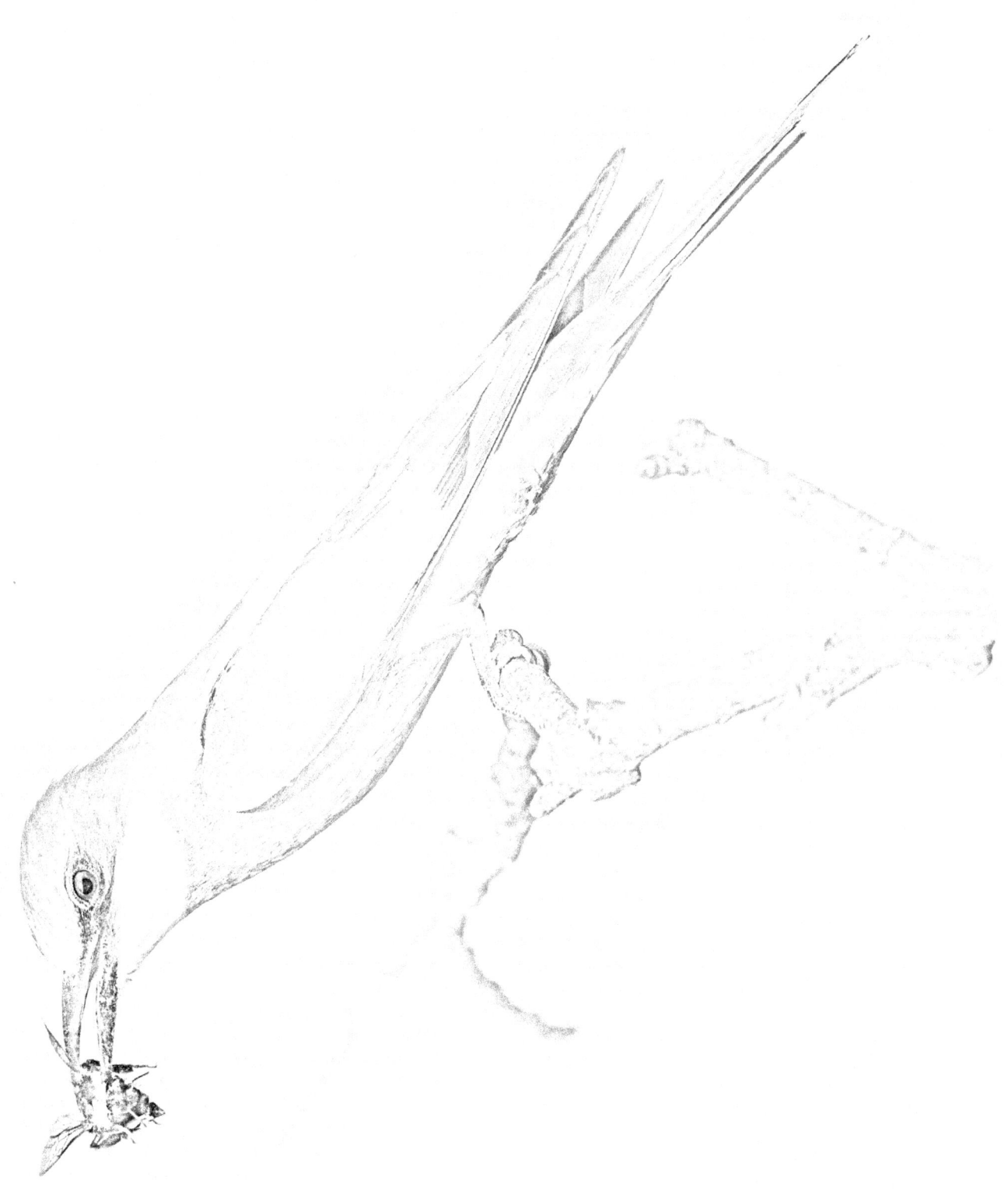

Merops apiaster - Female

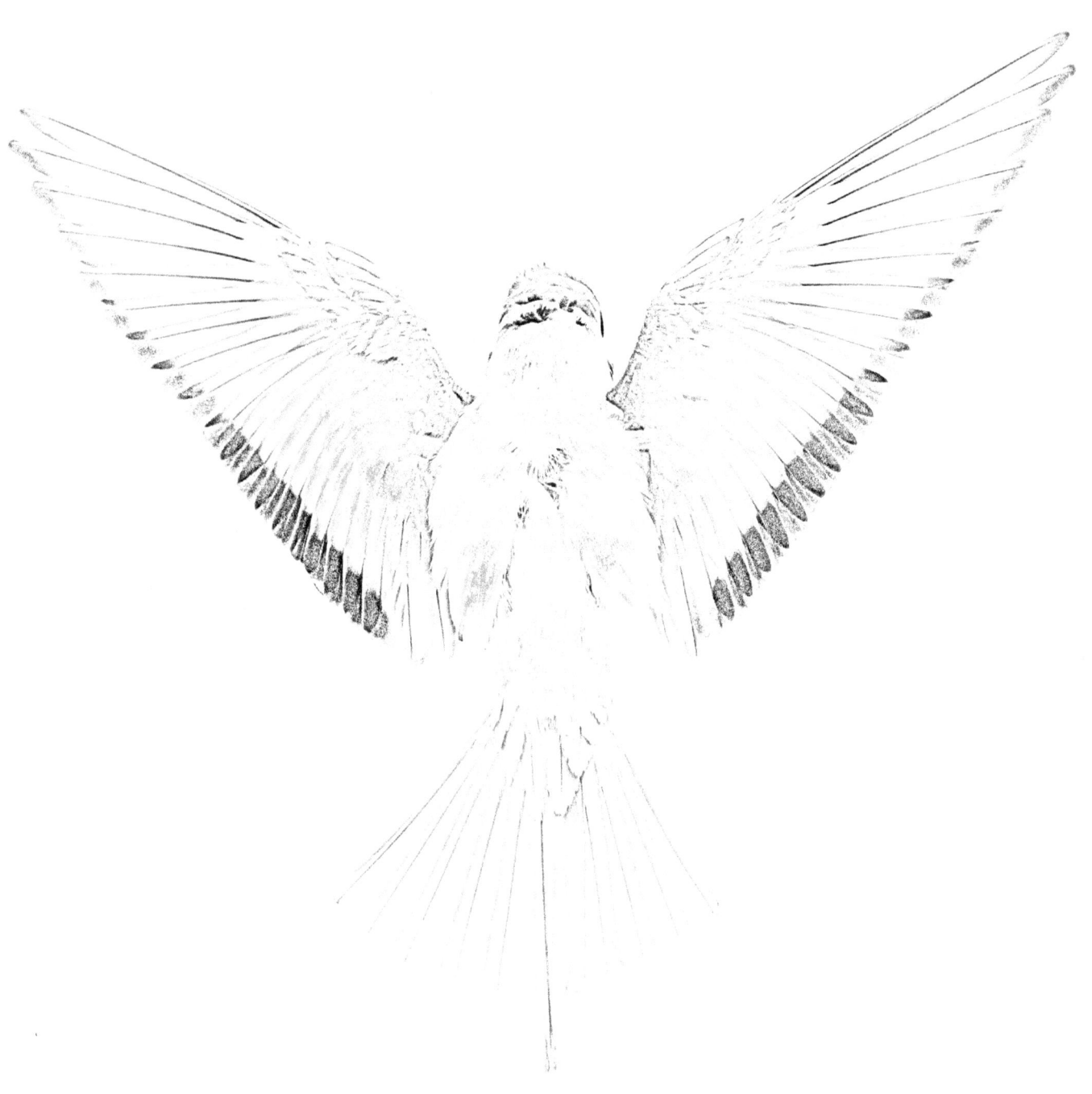

Emberiza schoeniclus - Female

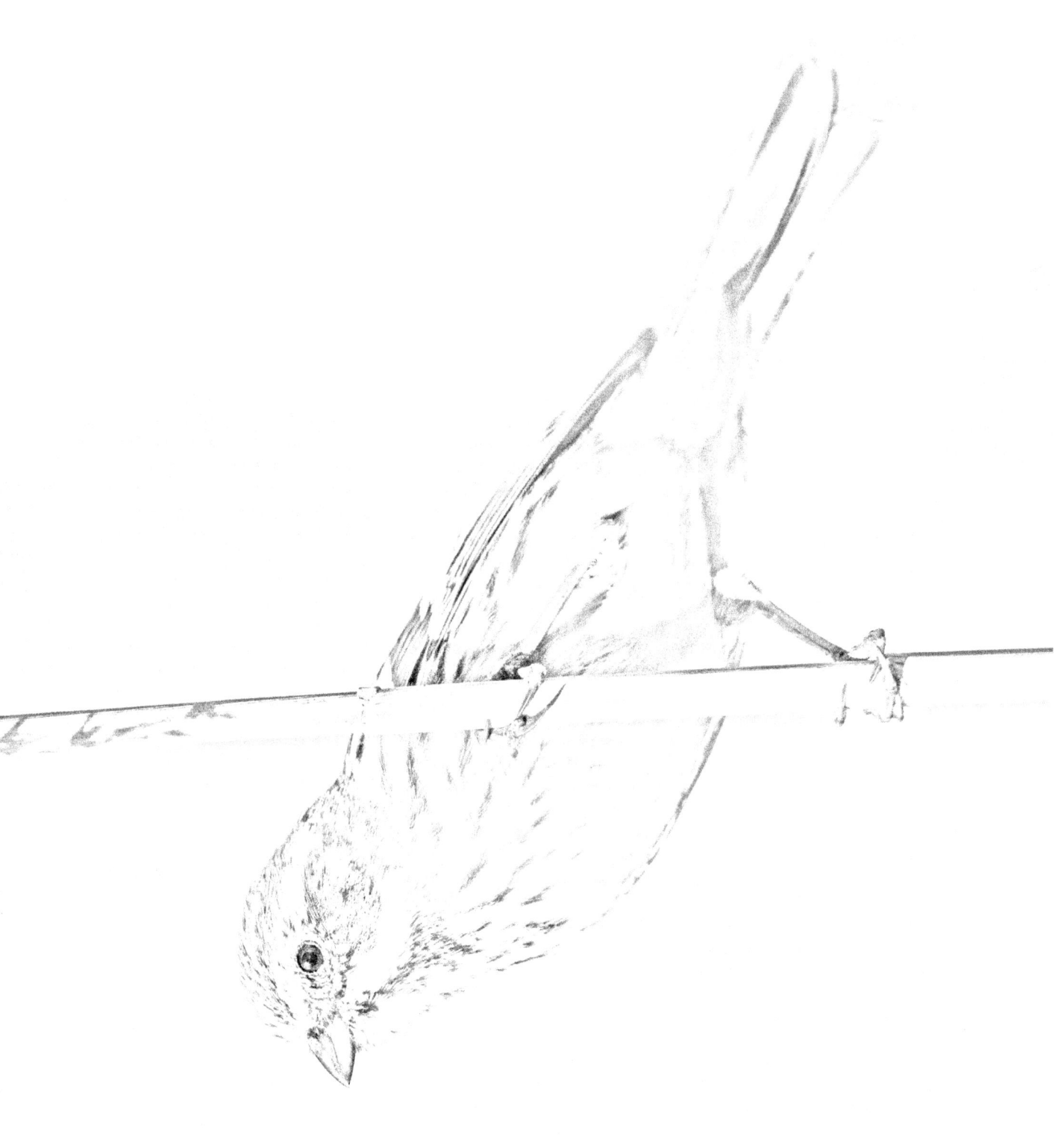

Passer domesticus -Female

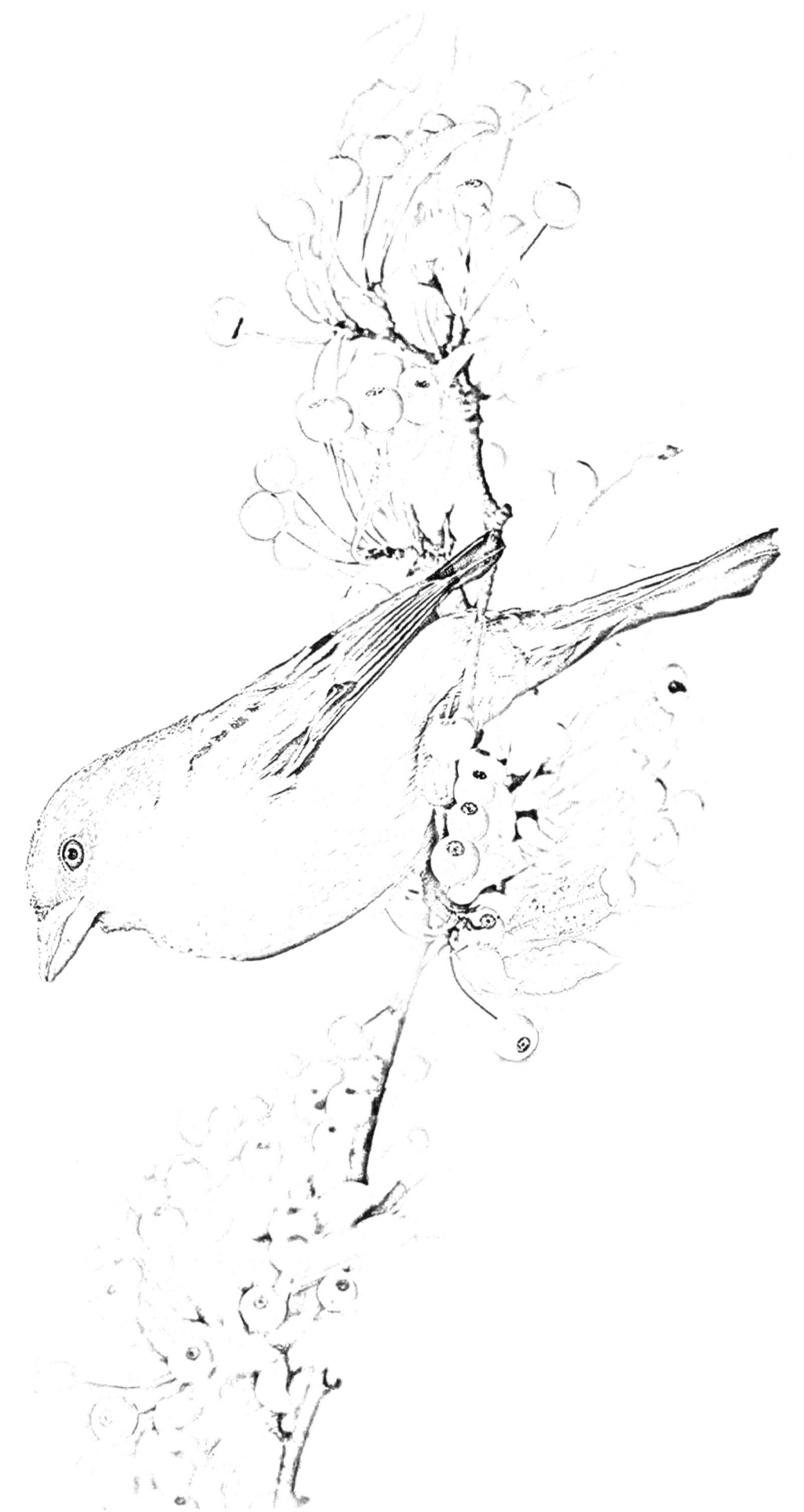

Sitta europaea - Male

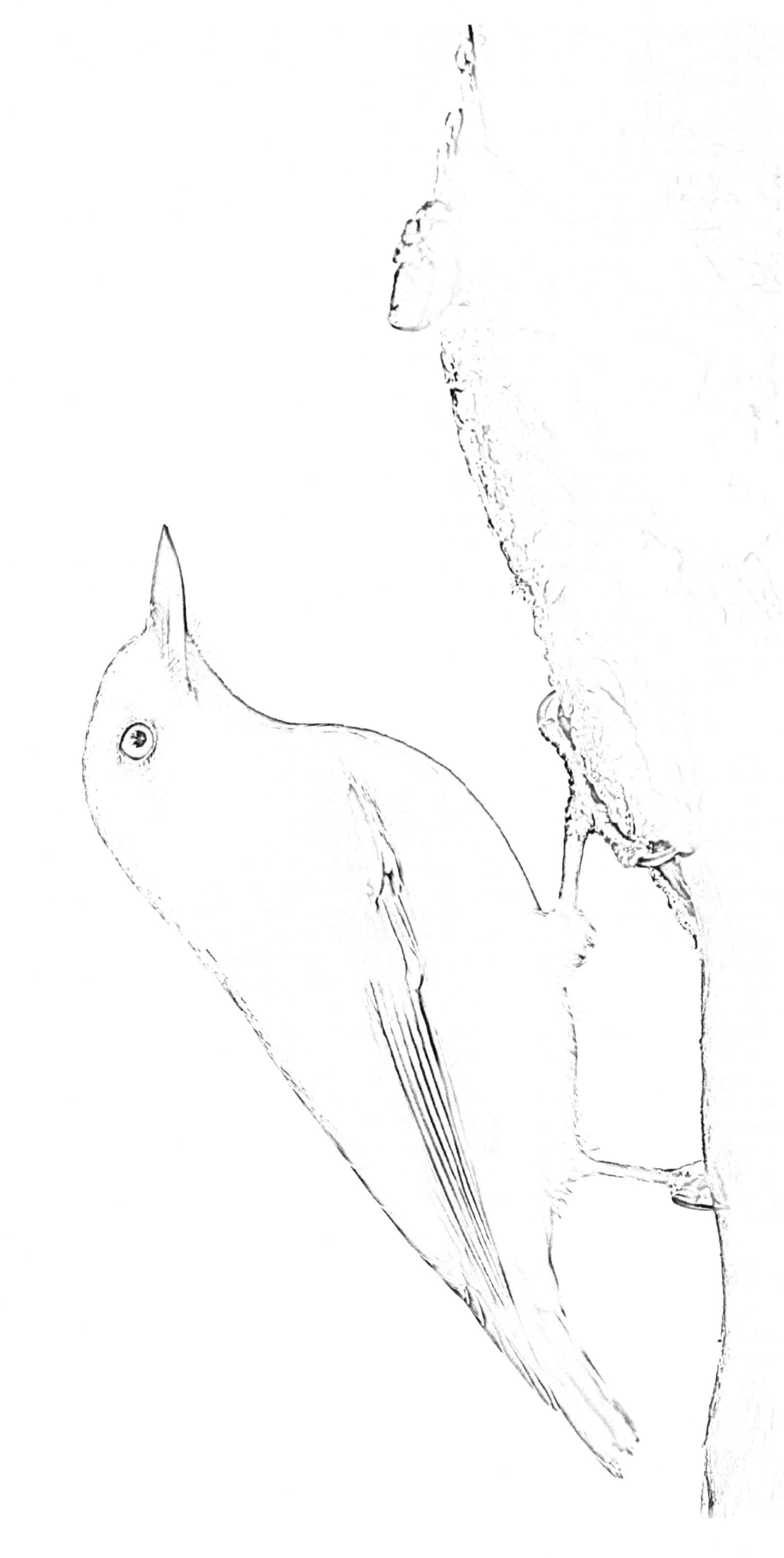

Sitta europaea - Male

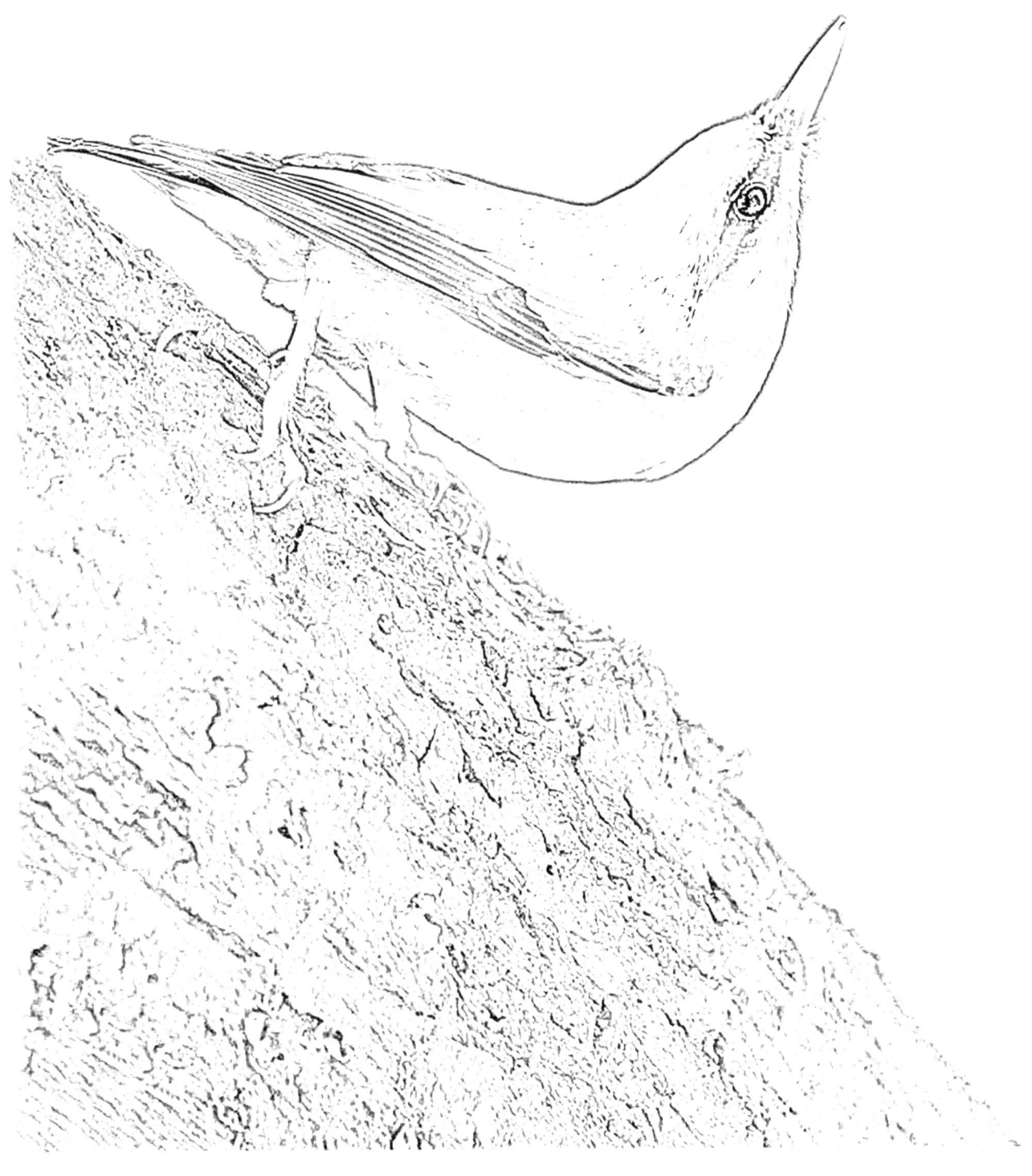

Regulus regulus - Male

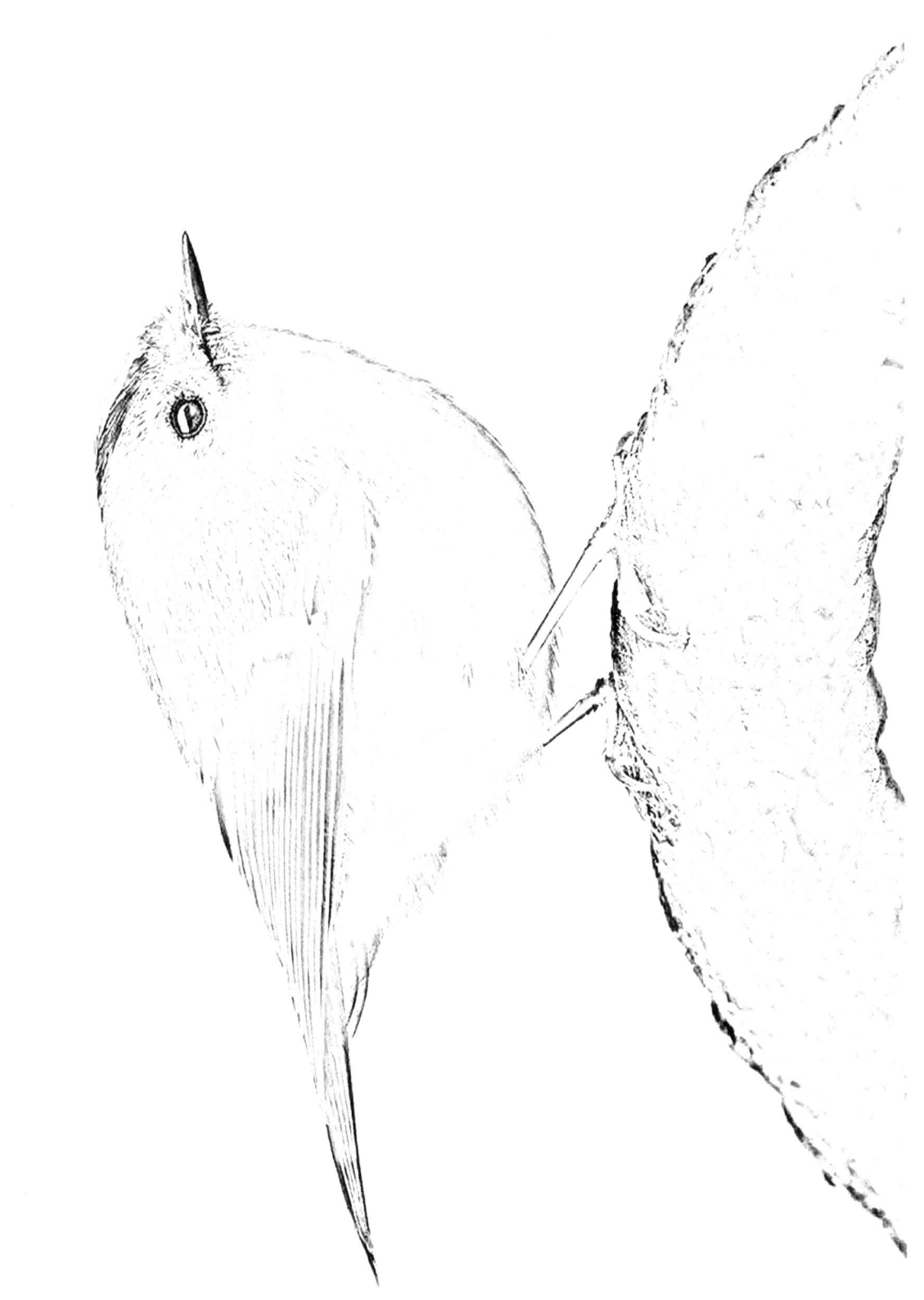

Erithacus rubecula - Male

Erithacus rubecula - Male

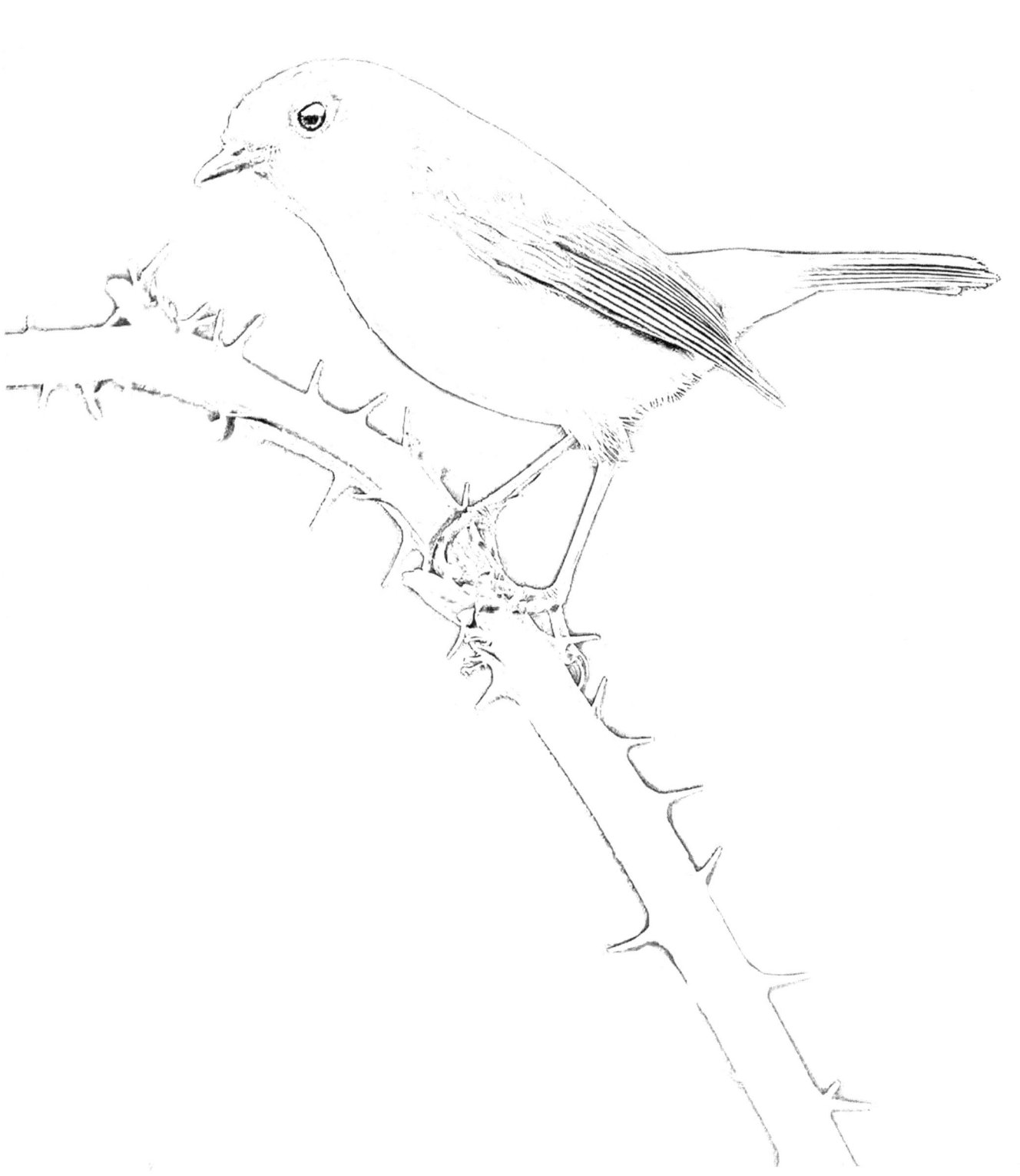

Hirundo rustica - Male

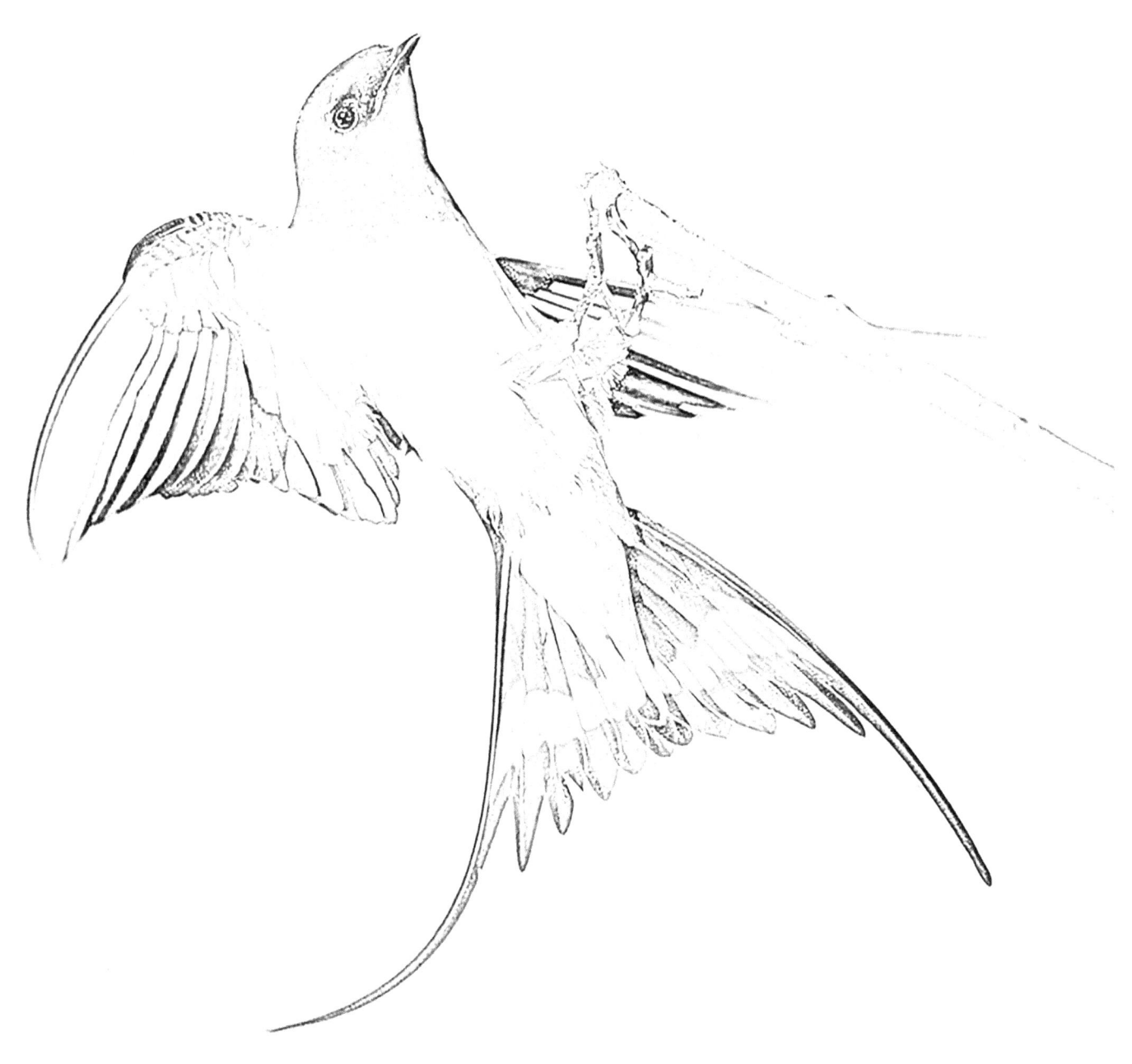

Saxicola torquatus - Male

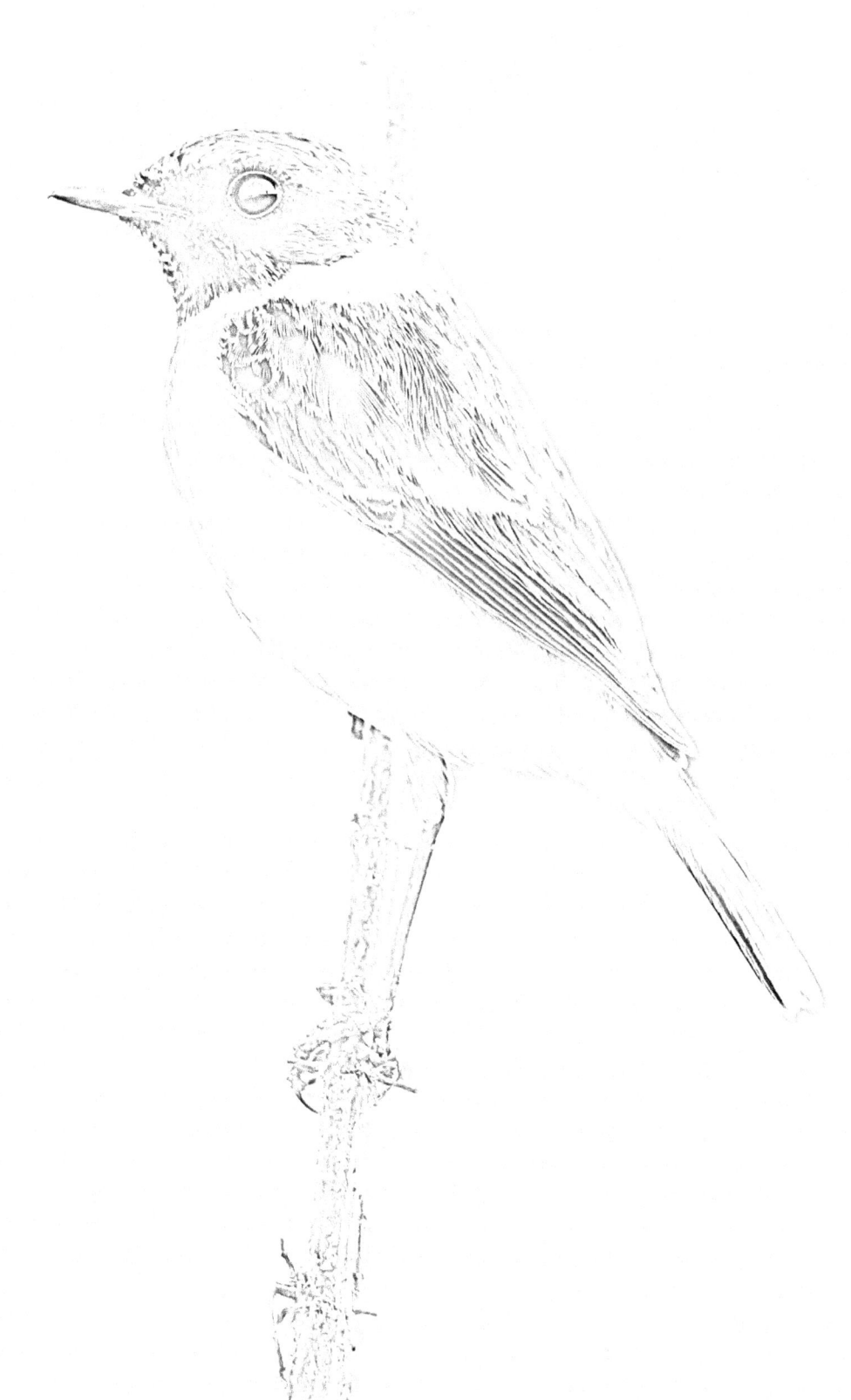

Saxicola rubetra - Female

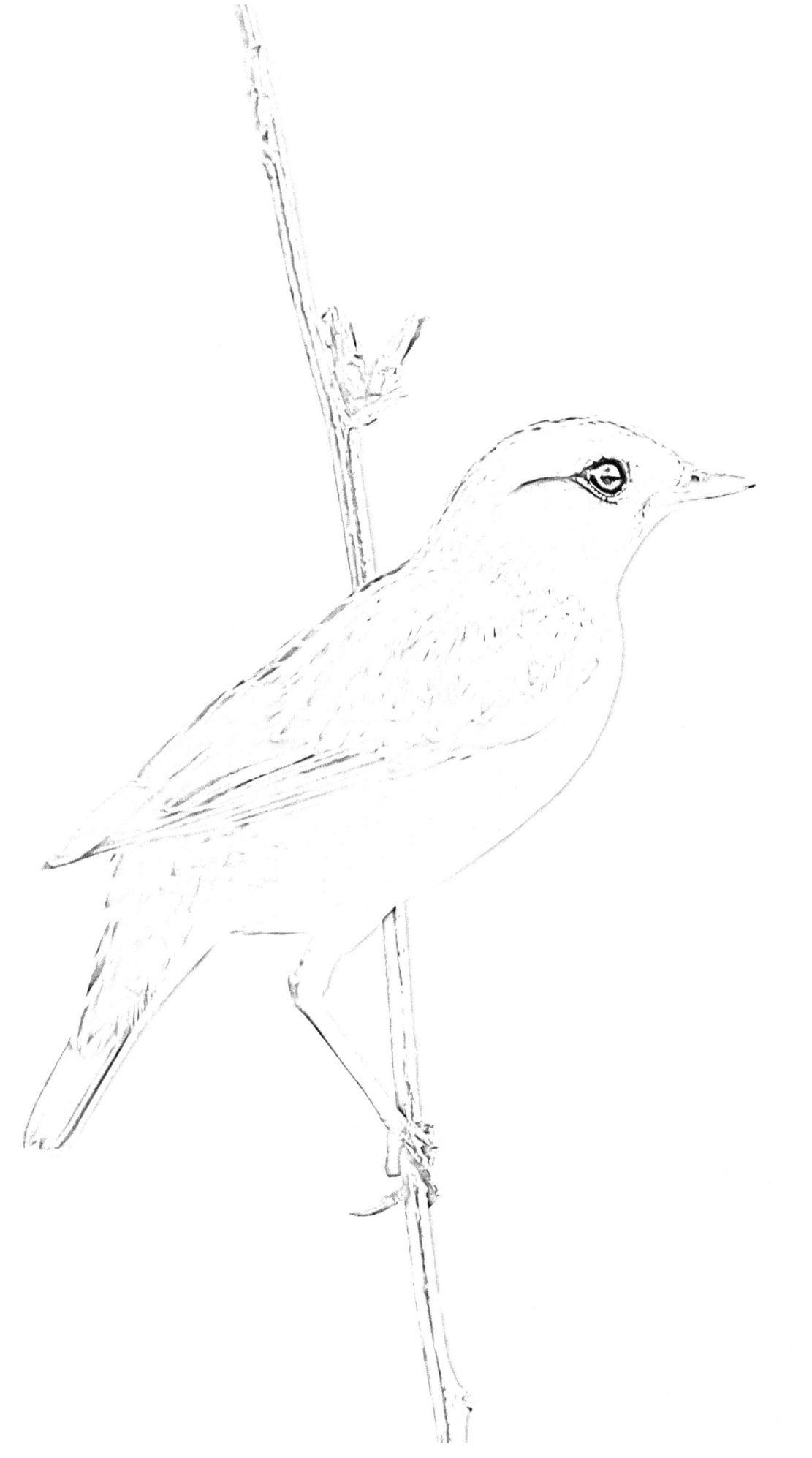

Saxicola rubetra - Male

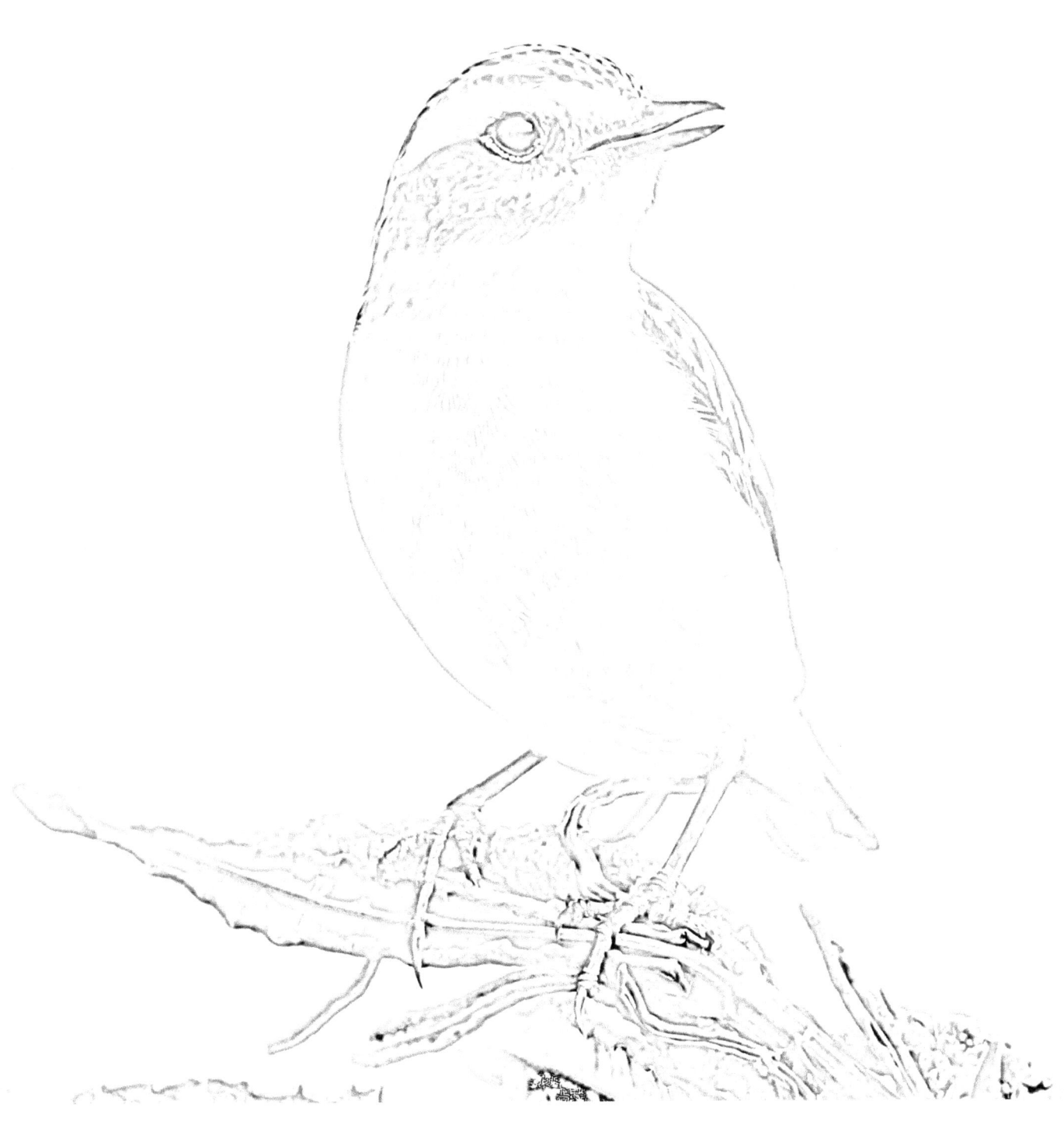

Sturnus vulgaris - Male

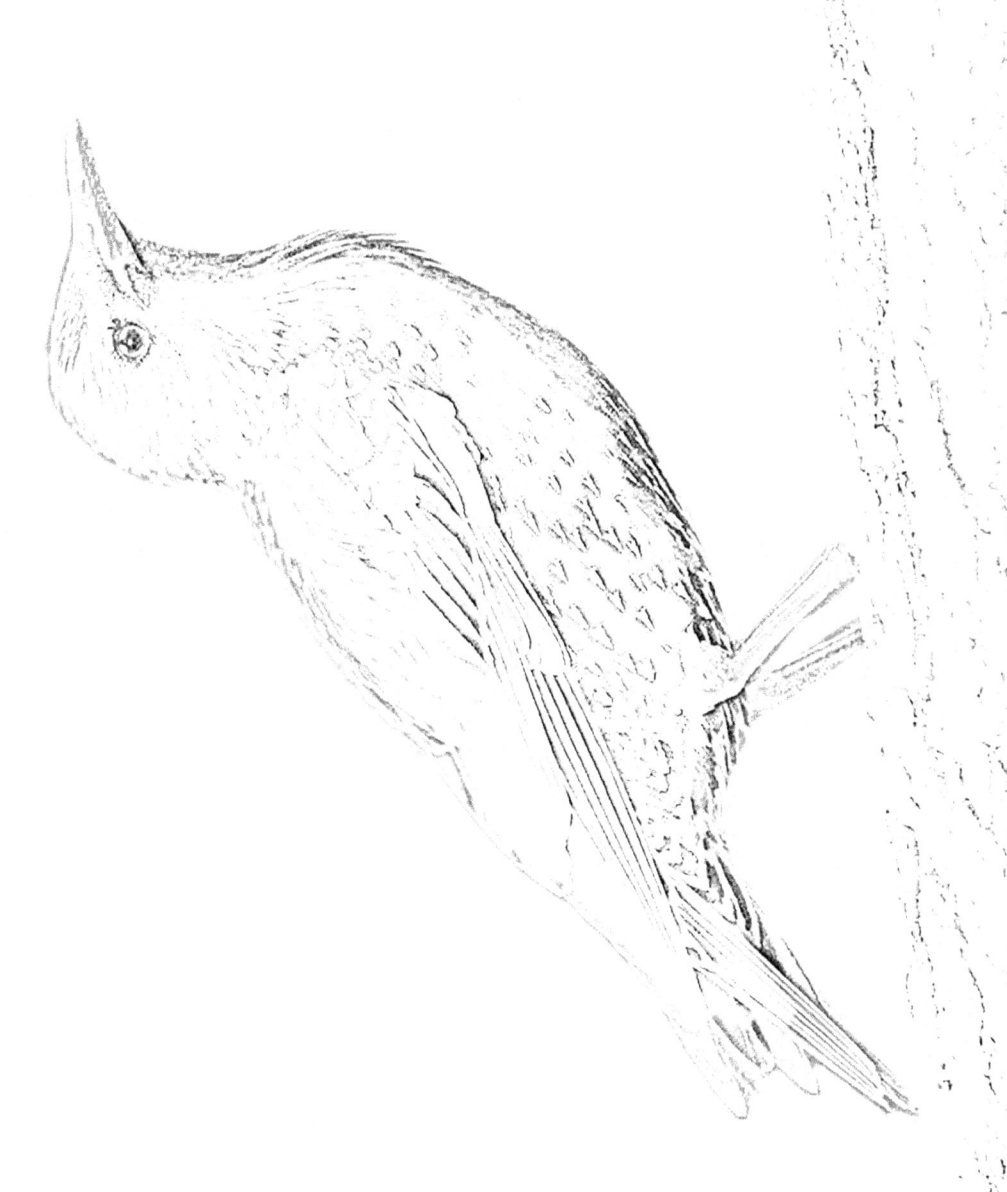

Jynx torquilla - Male

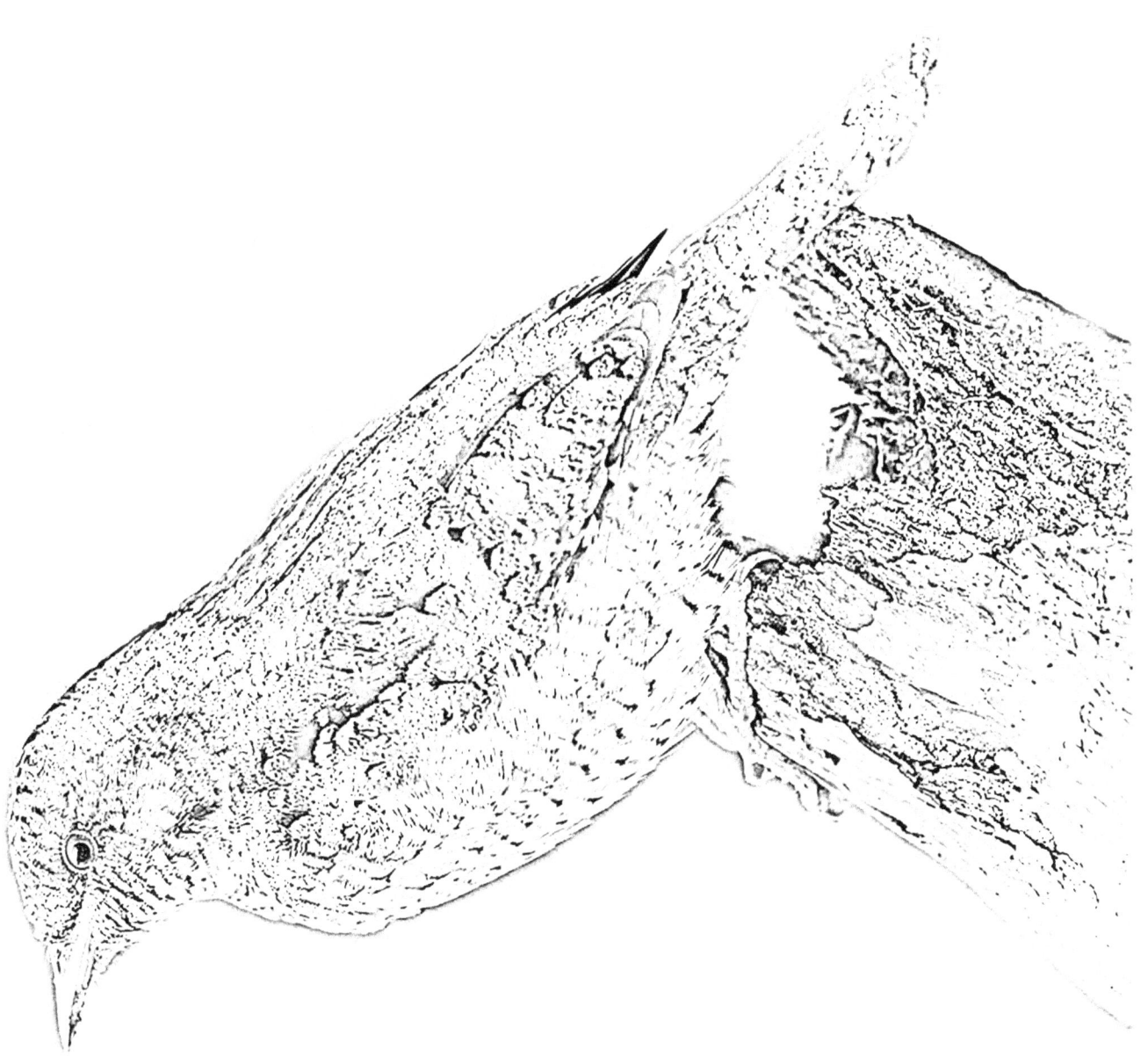

Chloris chloris - Male

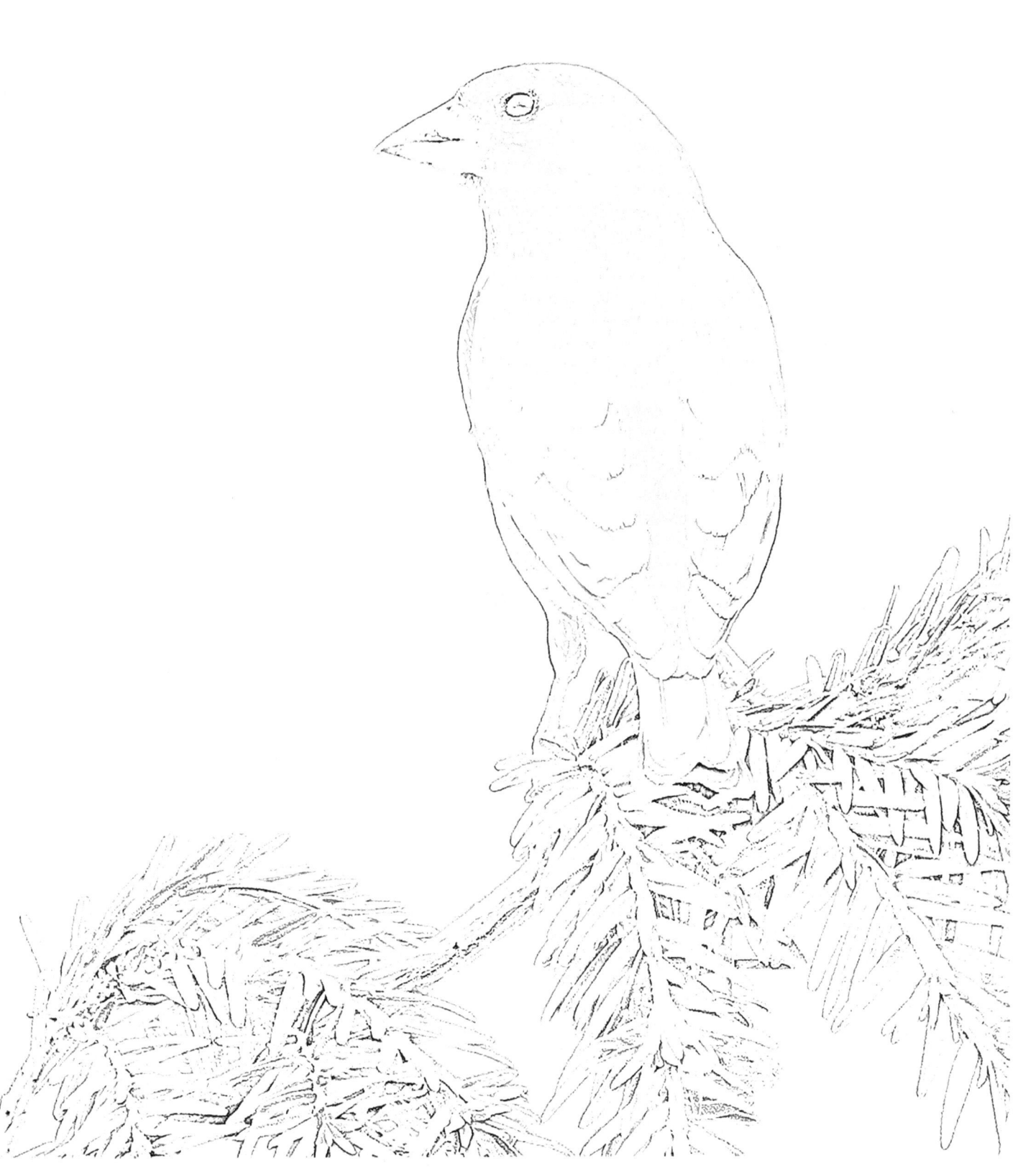

Chloris chloris - Male

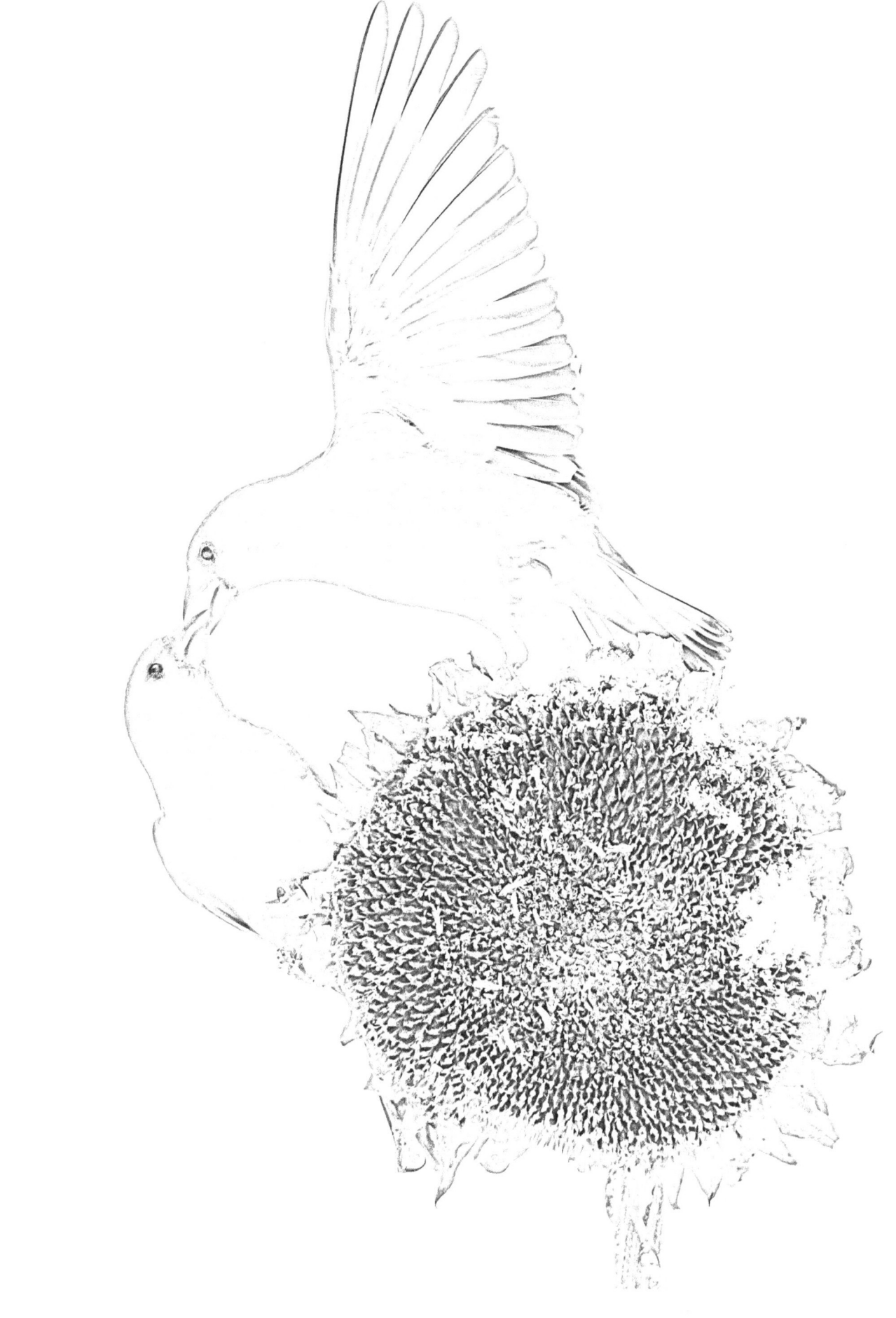

Thanks

Buying this book my art can live, also visit my social pages:

Instagram / Facebook / www.michelepietrangelo.com

Thank You.

All © right reserved by michelepietrangelo.com
Book desing, illustration, image, any ideas by Michele Pietrangelo
reproduction is prohibited without rights

www.ingramcontent.com/pod-product-compliance
Lightning Source LLC
Chambersburg PA
CBHW080459220526
45465CB00006B/2321